A STRAIGHTFORWARD
GUIDE
TO
EMPLOYMENT LAW

Karen Lee

Straightforward Guides
www.straightforwardco.co.uk

Straightforward Guides

British Library Cataloguing in Publication Data. A catalogue record for this book is available from the British Library.

ISBN

978-1-84716-878-8

Printed by 4edge www.4edge.co.uk
Series Editor: Roger Sproston

Cover design by Bookworks Islington

CONTENTS

Introduction

Introduction

It is hoped that this brief, but wide ranging, introduction to employment law, updated to **January 2019**, is accessible not only to the student or professional but also to the layperson. The book attempts to embrace the framework of employment law and up to date case law in various areas (where relevant) is introduced..

Throughout the book, there are cases, both current and historic, that serve to highlight main points of law. There is reference to the numerous Employment Acts and other relevant Acts. There is also a newly inserted chapter 2, which deals with the role of ACAS (Arbitration and Conciliation Service) in Employment law.

In December 2018, the government published its "good work plan", which is said to implement 50 out of the 53 recommendations of the Taylor Review, which was carried out in 2016 by Matthew Taylor, Chief Executive of the Royal Society of Arts. Mr Taylor was tasked with evaluating working practices in the UK over the past 20 to 30 years, and reporting on areas for reform. It was expected that a primary focus of the report would be the effect of the emerging "gig economy" on workers' rights. The report sets out a plethora of suggestions for reform, from employment status to tax reform,

It seems a long time since there has been any new employment law proposals, but this brings with it a wide range of proposed changes – mostly points of detail rather than major new initiatives, but even the points of detail are likely to be significant. For instance, a proposal to move the length of time needed to break continuous service from one week to four weeks, so that someone who works for an employer on a casual basis only once a month may be able to acquire the necessary length of service to claim unfair dismissal.

Other proposals including removing the 'Swedish derogation' from the Agency Worker Regulations, along with an enhanced entitlement to written particulars of employment starting from the first day of work and a right for casual workers to request a fixed working pattern. There will also be greater regulation of "umbrella" companies.

Almost every kind of employment relationship will be affected by these changes, if implemented. There are provisions for strengthening the enforcement of employment tribunal awards, including the possibility of penalties of up to £20,000 (rather than £5,000) and naming and shaming employers who do not pay employment tribunal awards.

The document is short on any timetable for implementing these proposed reforms, or when they may come into effect, and in the current political climate there may be issues with whether all or any these changes will make it through Parliament before an election.

The government is notably making the point in the document that these new proposals go further than required by EU law.

For further detail on the Good Work Plan go to www.gov.uk/government/news/millions-to-benefit-from-enhanced-rights-as-government-responds-to-taylor-review-of-modern-working-practices

****

Chapter 1

A Snapshot of The Main Areas of Employment Law

In this chapter, we will look, generally, at the main areas which cover employers and employees in the workplace, before covering specific areas of the law in the subsequent chapters..

The framework of employment law applies as soon as a job is applied for. Employers have legal obligations when drawing up a job description, specification and shortlist for a particular job. Essentially, prospective employers must not discriminate against a candidate on the grounds of age, sex, race, religion or disability. There are laws to prevent this. Nor can any other factor such as trade union membership serve to work against you.

Right to work checks
Employers must check that a job applicant is allowed to work for them in the UK before employing them. They must see the applicant's original documents. They must also check that the documents are valid with the applicant present. Finally they must make and keep copies of the documents and record the date they made the check. The employer could face a civil penalty if they employ an illegal worker and have not carried out a correct right to work check. The full guidance on carrying out right to work checks can be found at gov.uk/government/publications/right-to-work-checks-employers-guide

References prior to taking up a post.

Only certain industries such as those regulated by the Financial Services Authority are required to give a reference by law. Other employers do not have to give a reference but if they do it should be fair and accurate. Some employers may only give a factual reference stating dates of employment, job title and salary. Prospective employers must only approach a job applicant's current employer with the candidate's permission.

Prospective employers usually ask for references either prior to appointment or prior to interview. References vary but usually a previous employer should not provide a blatantly discriminatory reference which could jeopardise the chance of getting a job. However, they are under an obligation not to conceal certain facts, such as reasons for dismissal. The courts have taken the view that the duty is to provide a reference that is in substance true, accurate and fair. This was established in the key case of Spring v Guardian Assurance (1994) IRLR 460 where the complainant argued that a reference provided by a former employer was in breach of an implied term in the contract of employment that any reference would be compiled with all reasonable care. The House of Lords (now the Supreme Court) concluded that an employer has a duty to take reasonable care in compiling a reference by ensuring the accuracy of the information upon which it is based.

In another more recent case, Mefful v Citizens Advice Merton and Lambeth Limited 2015, an employee of eight years' standing was made redundant. While employed, he had two significant periods of absence - one for stress and grief, and the other for shoulder pain and total hearing loss in one ear.

He brought and won an unfair dismissal claim. A claim for disability discrimination was ongoing.

He applied for (and was offered) a new job, and his new employer asked his former employer for a reference, including whether there had been any absences from work (and why), and whether the former employer would re-employ him. It also asked other questions about his performance.

If an employer gives a reference, it has a duty to take reasonable care to ensure it is true, accurate and fair and that it is not misleading. This duty is owed to both the employee and to the new employer.

The former employer in this case gave information about the periods off work, but did not explain them. It said it would not re-employ him, and did not answer the other questions about his performance. The prospective employer withdrew the job offer because of the reference.

The employee successfully claimed victimisation and disability discrimination against his former employer. The Employment Tribunal (ET) found that:

- There had been a failure to explain the employee's periods of absence - to put them in a context, given his disability. They were also overstated.
- The manager providing the reference had a negative view of the employee because of his legal claims against the employer. The gaps in the reference were, in the ET's view, deliberate, and intended to show the employee in a bad light.
- The reference misrepresented the employee's eight years of employment, and was neither balanced nor fair.

In Summary

References can include:

- basic facts about the job applicant, like employment dates and job descriptions

- answers to questions that the potential employer has specifically asked about the job applicant that are not usually given as basic facts, like absence levels and confirming the reason for leaving

- details about the job applicant's skills and abilities

- details about the job applicant's character, strengths and weaknesses relating to the suitability for the role they have applied for

Previous employers will usually be asked to provide the basic facts and possibly answer some additional questions. However, previous managers and colleagues might also be asked to provide character details.

A reference must be a true, accurate and fair reflection of the job applicant. When opinions are provided, they should be based on facts.

Personal references can sometimes be provided from individuals who know the job applicant such as a teacher.

References should not include irrelevant personal information.

When are employment references needed?

References can be required at any stage of the recruitment process. Job applications should say if references will be required and at what stage of the recruitment process they will be needed.

Employers must only seek a reference from a job applicant's current employer with their permission.

Job offers and references

If a job applicant is offered a job there are two types of job offer that can be made:

- A **conditional** job offer. This can be withdrawn if the applicant doesn't meet the employer's condition for example, satisfactory references.

- An **unconditional** job offer. Once an unconditional offer is made this cannot be withdrawn and if accepted a contract is formed.

Once an employer has received satisfactory references and informed the job applicant an unconditional job offer can be made.

Employees should consider waiting until they get an unconditional offer before handing in their notice.

Immigration skills charge
Since April 2017, employers must now pay an Immigration Skills Charge of up to £1,000 per year for each skilled migrant they employ.

New regulations mean that employers must pay a fee, called the Immigration Skills Charge, for every skilled migrant they sponsor under the Tier 2 (General) or Tier 2 (Intra Company Transfer) categories. The fee per migrant is £1,000 per year for larger companies and a reduced rate of £364 for smaller companies.

It is the employer's responsibility to pay this fee, and failure to do so will mean that a certificate of sponsorship is invalid.

Applying for a job and application forms

When filling in an application form, it is clear that you should stick to the truth. In all cases, if it is found that you have lied when filling in an application form then that is a reason for dismissal. Few employers check educational qualifications and professional qualifications. This meant that in the past people were being employed to carry out jobs that they were not necessarily qualified to do. Companies now exist to check out CVs and application forms so honesty is the best policy.

Under the Immigration, Asylum and Nationality Act 2006 (which came into force on 29/2/2008), and which replaced the 1996 Immigration and Asylum Act, your employer must ask you for a National Insurance number or some evidence that you have the right to work in the UK. Employers have an obligation to carry out this check on all new employees. For employees who started work between 27/1/1996 and 28/2/2008 the 1996 Act applies. For full details of the kind of checks that need to be carried out and the sanctions against employers who do not comply visit the Home Office website on www.ukba.homeoffice.gov.uk.

Employers must also ask for criminal convictions. You do not have to reveal these if they are `spent'. This means that they happened long enough ago for the Rehabilitation of Offenders Act 1974 to allow you to keep them secret. If you are required to work with children or vulnerable adults, you will need to provide a certificate of disclosure. This is an official document which can be obtained from the Disclosure and Barring Service which has replaced the Criminal Records Bureau under the Protection of Freedoms Act 2012. It lists any relevant previous convictions More information about the Disclosures and Barring Service can be found on the Home Office website:
www.gov.uk/government/organisations/disclosure-and-barring-service.

Also, your prospective employer must check with the police that you have no convictions regarding children.

As soon as you have accepted a job, you will enter into a contract with your employer, even if you have received nothing in writing. The basic terms of offer and acceptance apply. See Chapter two for more details of contracts of employment.

Checking up on prospective employees on social media

Employers who use Facebook, Twitter and other social media to check on potential job candidates could be breaking European law in future. An EU data protection working party (Article 29) has ruled that employers should require "legal grounds" before snooping. The recommendations are non-binding, but will influence forthcoming changes to data protection laws. One Recruitment company suggests that 70% of employers use social networks to screen candidates. Its study also found that the same percentage are also using online search engines to research potential employees.

Guidelines

The guidelines from the Article 29 working party informed a radical shake-up of European data protection laws, known as the General Data Protection Regulation (GDPR), which came into force in May 2018. Their recommendations also suggest that any data collected from an internet search of potential candidates must be necessary and relevant to the performance of the job. The general rules are that employers should inform applicants if they are going to look at social media profiles and give them the opportunity to comment. The searches should also be proportionate to the job being applied for. Implementation of the GDPR might tighten the enforcement of such guidelines. See further on in this chapter for more about GDPR effective from May 2018.

20

Other rights in the workplace

There are many rights (and obligations) at work, which begin from the day your employment commences. These are covered in depth throughout this book. To summarise a few of the fundamental areas:

Time off for public and workforce duties

All employees are entitled to reasonable time off to perform public duties, including serving as a magistrate or a local authority councillor. Your contract of employment may give you a right to paid time off for such duties. In addition, trade union representatives, union learning representatives, company pension trustees and designated health and safety representatives are also entitled to paid time off work to carry out duties.

Losing or leaving a job

There are two types of notice period: statutory and contractual. Statutory notice is the minimum legal notice that can be given. Employers should give the employee:

- **one week's notice** if the employee has been employed by the employer continuously for one month or more, but for less than two years

- **two weeks' notice** if the employee has been employed by the employer continuously for two years, and one additional week's notice for each further complete year of continuous employment, up to a maximum of 12 weeks. For example if an employee has worked for 5 years then they are entitled to 5 weeks' notice.

Employees must give their employer a minimum of one week's notice once they have worked for one month. This minimum is unaffected by longer service.

21

However, contractual notice is the amount of notice that the employer can set out in the terms and conditions of employment which can be longer than the statutory notice. For example the statutory notice an employee must give to an employer is one week, however, an employer can state within the terms of employment that an employee must give one month's notice.

Dismissal without notice

In a few cases employers may dismiss someone without notice on the grounds of gross misconduct. Gross misconduct occurs when an employee has committed a serious act such as theft, violence, physical abuse, serious breach in health and safety or gross negligence. Employers should give employees a clear indication of the type of issues that could constitute gross misconduct, and it is still important to follow a fair procedure as for any other disciplinary offence.

Fixed term contracts

Generally, no notice of the expiry of a fixed-term contract will need to be given, however, if the contract is terminated by giving notice before its expiry date then the correct amount of statutory notice should be given.

Failure by the employer to give the correct notice period may amount to a breach of contract and employees may make a claim to an employment tribunal.

The *Unfair Dismissal and Statement of Reasons for Dismissal (Variation of Qualifying Period) Order 2012* increased the qualifying period for the right to claim unfair dismissal to **two years** for employees whose employment commenced on or after 6 April 2012. Before this, section 108 of the *Employment Rights Act 1996* provided that employees had to have been continuously employed by their employer for at least **one year** to claim protection against unfair dismissal. In a variety of unfair dismissal cases specified by legislation, particular reasons for dismissal will be "automatically unfair". In these cases there is normally no requirement for a continuous period of employment.

You'll need to check quickly - you've got 3 months less a day from the date you were sacked to start taking action for an unfair dismissal.

If you change your mind

If you resign in the 'heat of the moment' (eg during an argument) and you change your mind, you should tell your employer immediately. They can choose to accept your resignation or not.

Payment during notice period

You're entitled to your normal pay rate during your notice period, including when you're:

- off sick
- on holiday
- temporarily laid off
- on maternity, paternity or adoption leave
- available to work, even if your employer has nothing for you to do

'Payment in lieu' of notice period

Your employer can ask you to leave immediately after handing in your notice. If they do, they'll probably offer you a one-off payment instead of allowing you to work out your notice period - called 'payment in lieu'. You can only get payment in lieu if it's in your contract, or if you agree to it. If you don't agree to it, you can work out your notice period.

Gardening leave

Your employer may ask you not to come into work, or to work at home or another location during your notice period. This is called 'gardening leave'. You'll get the same pay and contractual benefits.

Relocation of work

If your employer moves the location of their business, your situation depends firstly on the terms of your contract of employment. Some contracts include a mobility clause which says you have to move within certain limits. The notice period to move has to be reasonable as do all the other aspects of moving. You may decide not to move because of increased travel time and costs, moving house, family situation or children's education. If you don't have a mobility clause in your contract, and the relocation is more than a short distance, you can decide not to move. In this case, your employer may make you redundant. See Chapter 6, Being Made Redundant. When you are facing redundancy there is a right to a trial period in any alternative job that you have been offered. Redundancy is a dismissal so if you feel badly treated you may be able to claim for unfair dismissal.

If your employer decides to relocate:

- Check your contract of employment to see if there is a mobility clause
- Find out whether your employer is offering a relocation package and, if so, whether you think it is reasonable
- Discuss the matter of moving with your employer and state your intentions. If you decide to move talk to your employer about a trial period in the job
- If you decide not to relocate and your employer considers that you are being unreasonable and refuses you a redundancy payment, you can take the matter to an

Employment Tribunal (see Chapter 9) for them to decide whether you or your employer are being unreasonable. Note that fees apply.

Public and bank holidays

There is no statutory right to public and bank holidays as paid leave. This will generally be incorporated in your contract. Your employer may also count public and bank holidays as part of your annual leave. This is legal under the Working Time Regulations 1998 (see further in this book).

Transfer of a business

If your company is taken over, or if you work for the public sector and your job is transferred to the private sector, your terms and conditions of employment transfer automatically to the new employer, subject to conditions. Continuity of employment is guaranteed. You have the right to raise objections about your contract being transferred to another company. However, this can he fraught with problems.

The transfer of contracts is known generally as the transfer of undertakings, covered by the Transfer of Undertakings (Protection of Employment) Regulations 2006, as amended by the Collective Redundancies and Transfer of Undertakings (Protection of Employment) (Amendment) Regulations 2014 and is complex. Refer to the chapter on redundancy for more information. If you have a problem you will certainly need specialist advice from a union or other advice agency.

Sunday working

Certain groups of workers have protection in relation to working on a Sunday. They include shop workers and people who work in the betting industry. The aim was to allow those who do not wish to work on a Sunday to resist pressure to do so. However, if you have agreed a contract of employment that says you will work on Sunday then you do not have protection. Only employees who work in the above occupations have protection. For all other occupations, Sunday is just another day. There is also no legal right to extra pay for work on a Sunday although most contracts of employment will incorporate agreed overtime rates.

Insolvency of employer

If your employer goes bankrupt and cannot pay wages, the state will make up at least part of the pay. You can claim for statutory redundancy pay, for up to eight weeks. As well as basic wages you can claim any holiday pay up to 6 weeks, unpaid pension contributions and the basic award for unfair dismissal. You must apply to the employer's representative, usually the liquidator or receiver. You will be given a form which you should fill in and send off to the address on the form. HMRC will pay you any statutory sick pay, statutory maternity pay, statutory paternity pay and statutory adoption pay.

Suspension on medical grounds

In certain situations, usually for health and safety reasons, employers may feel obliged to suspend an employee from work on medical grounds. There are certain regulations under which medical suspension can apply - these usually involve working with chemicals or radioactive material or lead. There are also certain regulations in the Food Preparation industry which might lead to a suspension. This is because your Employer feels that you are a danger to your fellow employees!

Finally, if a pregnant woman is not able to carry out her normal duties, and no suitable alternative work can be provided, she can also be medically suspended from work.

If you are suspended from work on medical grounds in line with one of the qualifying regulations or conditions, then you are entitled to full pay for up to 26 weeks (as long as you have at least 1 months service). Any dismissal during this protected period is unfair. This does not apply if you are physically or mentally unfit for work. (If this is the case you will be entitled to some sick pay). It purely means that you are not capable of carrying out certain activities due to your condition. If you are offered suitable alternative work but refuse this, then no payment may be due to you. If your employer does not pay you, you can take a claim to an employment Tribunal, within three months.

Employment through agencies

Whereas once agency employment was tenuous, to say the least, all agency workers have some degree of protection under the 1973 Agencies Act. Legislation which came into effect from 1st October 2011 (Agency Workers Regulations 2010) has strengthened these rights. If you are working for an employment agency you may or may not be legally an employee. At the very least you will be a worker hired out to an employer to perform a service. Whether or not you are an employee, agency workers have basic rights:

All agency workers are covered by health and safety law, where the agency has a responsibility not to place you in a job for which you are not appropriately qualified and the company hiring you has a responsibility for providing a healthy and safe working environment.

-All agencies, and therefore agency workers, are covered by discrimination law, which also covers the hiring company.

-All agency workers are entitled to be paid the National Minimum Wage.

-All agency workers are entitled not to work more than an average of 48 hours a week unless you sign an agreement with the agency to the contrary.
-All agency workers should receive five weeks and three days paid annual leave once you have worked for more than 12 weeks.

Some agencies have been circumventing this by saying that your pay includes holiday pay and that they therefore do not have to pay extra if you take a break. It is unclear as to whether this is legal or not. As an agency worker you may also be entitled to statutory maternity pay or paternity pay, depending on your earnings and how long you have worked for the agency. You are also allowed to join a union.

If you are an agency worker and you accept a permanent post then you are expected to work out a period of notice as an agency temp before becoming permanent. The company can also agree to pay the employer a lump sum to release you from your contract.

Other basic protections for agency workers are:
-You have the right to be paid by your agency, on the agreed day, even if the hiring company has not paid the agency.
-You must be consulted before any changes are made to the terms of employment or terms and conditions of employment.

For a full resume of rights you should visit :
www.citizensadvice.org.uk/work/rights-at-work/agency-workers/additional-rights-for-agency-workers/. This is the Citizens Advice website.

Trade Union rights
A person has the right to decide whether they want to join a trade union or not. Employers are not entitled to know whether they are

in a union. They should certainly not be asked questions at an interview about union membership, views or activity. Since 2004, Employers have not been allowed to offer incentives to an employee to leave a union, for example a higher pay rise to non-union employees.

If a person thinks they have been turned down for a job, or overlooked for promotion, because of their union membership or activity they should take further advice as this is a form of discrimination which is unlawful. The same applies if they think that they have been dismissed due to union membership or union activity. A special level of compensation is available for this.

A person can join any union of their choice, but obviously it is sensible to join a union which represents workers in specific jobs.

Employers only have to deal with a union if that union is formally "recognised" by the employer. This is a legal process which the union has to go through to get certain rights and protection. Views are more likely to be considered by an employer when the union is "recognised" by an employer.

Where the union is "recognised", the employer is legally obliged to discuss certain matters with the union, such as pay and terms of employment. Redundancy is another area that employers must consult the union on.

In certain circumstances a person is entitled to time off work for union meetings - but the employer does not have to pay when attending a union meeting. Some employers do give some paid time off to attend a union meeting, particularly when those meetings are important - pay offers or redundancy terms for example.

Representation

All workers now have the right to have a representative with them during formal disciplinary or grievance meetings. This can be a union rep but does not have to be. A person has the right to have a union rep with them even if the employer does not recognise any union. This is a right.

Trade Union Officials

As an elected representative of a trade union a person becomes entitled to certain rights and protection. A person can take paid time off to attend training courses and carry out union duties for example.

Strike action

Employees enjoy some protection if they go on official strike action called by a trade union. This protected period was increased to 12 weeks from October 2004, and it can be longer in certain situations - where an employer has made no attempt to negotiate, or employees have been "locked out" by an employer are examples. A person is not protected against dismissal if they take unofficial strike action. See the section in Chapter 10, Trade Unions, about the Trade Unions Act 2016, which became effective in March 2017 and which affects the rights to strike..

Whistleblowing

The general duty that confidential information must not be disclosed has always been subject to an important common law exception, that disclosure may be justified when it is in the public interest. The Public Interest Disclosure Act 1998 introduced new sections into the Employment Rights Act 1996 making it automatically unfair to dismiss workers or subject them to any detriment where they have made a protected disclosure. as reflected in changes to the regulations coming into effect on 25th June 2013,disclosure of information is only protected where the worker honestly believes on reasonable grounds that it tends to show that a criminal offence is being committed, there has been

30

failure to comply with a legal obligation, a miscarriage of justice has taken place, there is a danger to health and safety at work, damage to the environment or the deliberate concealment of any of these. An important case in this area is Chesterton Global Ltd and Nurmohamed (Court of Appeal) 2017. In this case, an estate agent raised concerns of accounting malpractice, which he alleged were designed to reduce the amount of commission paid to around 100 senior managers, including himself. The Court of Appeal had to decide if the estate agents disclosure 'was in the public interest' a key requirement for statutory whistle blowing protection. The Court held that the estate agents disclosure satisfied the 'public interest' requirement despite the concerns affecting the company's staff only and the whistleblower's personal interest in the issue.

The Data Protection Act

Privacy at work is an issue which is gaining more prominence. Employers are in a position to collect increasing amounts of data about employees. The Data Protection Act 2018, which is the UK's implementation of the General Data Protection Regulations (GDPR) (see below) provides some important rights which people should be aware of. This Act gives Employees some control over information that their employer holds over them.

The Act gives all workers the right to be told about the type of information their employer holds over them, how that information is to be used and about anyone else with access to it. The employer must ensure that all information kept is confidential. Certain types of data, such as information about sexuality and religion cannot be kept. Employers can hold or use such sensitive data only in certain situations, such as when required to do so by law.

You have the right to see a copy of any information held about you. The Regulations cover data kept on electronic or paper files. You can expect to see personnel files and other information held on file about you. The legislation also allows you to see reference information provided about you. An employer has an obligation to provide information promptly and can require a worker to pay a fee of up to £10 for producing the information.

An employee can refuse to disclose information if it means putting at risk a third party or requires disproportionate effort.

If any problems are experienced in this area there is the right to make a complaint to the information commissioner's office.

The General Data Protection Regulation (GDPR) (Regulation (EU) 2016/679)

It is important for employers and employees to note that the rules surrounding data protection have been tightened. The GDPR is a regulation by which the European Parliament, the Council of the European Union and the European Commission intend to strengthen and unify data protection for all individuals within the European Union (EU). It also addresses the export of personal data outside the EU. The GDPR aims primarily to give control back to citizens and residents (employees) over their personal data and to simplify the regulatory environment for international business by unifying the regulation within the EU. The GDPR replaces the data protection directive (officially Directive 95/46/EC) of 1995. The regulation was adopted on 27 April 2016. It became enforceable on 25 May 2018 after a two-year transition period and, unlike a directive, it does not require national governments to pass any enabling legislation, and is thus directly binding and applicable. As mentioned above, The Data Protection Act 2018 is the UK's implementation of the General Data Protection Regulations.

Monitoring at work

Most employers will carry out some form of monitoring in relation to their employees and this is accepted. However, where monitoring goes beyond the accepted boundaries of employee performance it needs to be done in a way that is lawful and fair. The Information Commissioner has set out guidance for employers in the Employment Practice Data Protection Code. Although the code is not a legal obligation itself, if your employer is not adhering to it he or she may be breaking the law on which it is based. For more information on the code of practice you can visit the website of the Information Commissioner at:

www.informationcommissioner.gov.uk

In Summary, The Data Protection Act 2018 lays out that:

Everyone responsible for using personal data has to follow strict rules called 'data protection principles'. They must make sure the information is:

- used fairly, lawfully and transparently
- used for specified, explicit purposes
- used in a way that is adequate, relevant and limited to only what is necessary
- accurate and, where necessary, kept up to date
- kept for no longer than is necessary
- handled in a way that ensures appropriate security, including protection against unlawful or unauthorised processing, access, loss, destruction or damage

There is stronger legal protection for more sensitive information, such as:

- race
- ethnic background
- political opinions
- religious beliefs
- trade union membership
- genetics
- biometrics (where used for identification)
- health, sex life or orientation

There are separate safeguards for personal data relating to criminal convictions and offences.

Your rights

Under the Data Protection Act 2018, you have the right to find out what information the government and other organisations store about you. These include the right to:

- be informed about how your data is being used
- access personal data
- have incorrect data updated
- have data erased
- stop or restrict the processing of your data
- data portability (allowing you to get and reuse your data for different services)
- object to how your data is processed in certain circumstances

You also have rights when an organisation is using your personal data for:

- automated decision-making processes (without human involvement)

- profiling, for example to predict your behaviour or interests

Use of Social media in the workplace
Overview

Social media is the term used for internet-based tools used on computer, tablets, and smart phones to help people keep in touch and enable them to interact. It allows people to share information, ideas and views. Social media can affect communications among managers, employees and job applicants; how organisations promote and control their reputation; and how colleagues treat one another. It can also distort what boundaries there are between home and work.

Some estimates report that misuse of the internet and social media by workers costs Britain's economy billions of pounds every year and add that many employers are already grappling with issues like time theft, defamation, cyber bullying, freedom of speech and the invasion of privacy.

Legal considerations

The Human Rights Act 1998 Article 8 gives a 'right to respect for private and family life, home and correspondence'. Case law suggests that employees have a reasonable expectation of privacy in the workplace.

The Data Protection Act 1988 (as amended) covers how information about employees and job applicants can be collected, handled and used. The Information Commissioner's Office has published an employment practices code.

The Regulation of Investigatory Powers Act 2000 covers the extent to which organisations can use covert surveillance.

35

Developing a policy

Employers should develop a policy setting out what is and what is not acceptable behaviour at work when using the internet, emails, smart phones, and networking websites. The policy should also give clear guidelines for employees on what they can and cannot say about the organisation. Any policy should be clear throughout about the distinction between business and private use of social media. If it allows limited private use in the workplace, it should be clear what this means in practice.

In working out a policy for use of social media, the employer, staff and unions or staff reps (if there are any) should agree the details. The policy should aim to ensure: employees do not feel gagged; staff and managers feel protected against online bullying; and the organisation feels confident its reputation will be guarded.

Disciplinary procedures

An employer should try to apply the same standards of conduct in online matters as it would in offline issues. To help an organisation respond reasonably, the employer should consider the nature of the comments made and their likely impact on the organisation. It would help if the employer gives examples of what might be classed as 'defamation' and the penalties it would impose. The employer should also be clear in outlining what is regarded as confidential in the organisation.

Blogging and tweeting

If an employee is representing the company online, the employer should set appropriate rules for what information they may disclose and the range of opinions they may express. Bring to their attention relevant legislation on copyright and public interest disclosure. Some rules should be included on the use of social media in recruitment, which managers and employees should follow. When

36

recruiting, employers should be careful if assessing applicants by looking at their social networking pages - this can be discriminatory and unfair.

Using email at work

Email is an integral part of many peoples working lives. An organisation should have clear rules on how staff use their work email, whether it may be monitored and if there are time limits for deleting emails no longer required for business purposes. Additionally, an organisation may want to provide guidance for staff on how to make the best use of email and ensure that it does not place unnecessary stress and pressure on them. Research commissioned by Acas suggested organisations may benefit from providing staff with email management strategies to help effectively manage inboxes. Other areas identified in the research included encouraging staff to use the 'delay send' function when sending an email out-of-hours. This means that colleagues receive the email during normal working hours rather than at home, which can adversely affect their work-life balance.

Language requirements in the workplace

Language requirements can be a legal minefield. Although customer-facing public sector staff must be fluent in English, the legal position for private companies wanting to introduce a similar policy is less clear.

Regulations made under the Immigration Act 2016 that came into effect on 22 December 2016 brought into force the Code of Practice and introduced the requirement for public sector workers who speak to the public as a regular and intrinsic part of their role to be fluent in English (and English or Welsh in Wales). There is no equivalent fluency requirement for the private sector.

Imposing language requirements

While employers are generally free to draw up their own requirements for roles within their business, they should not breach their duties under the Equality Act 2010 by discriminating against those with a 'protected characteristic'.

Whereas businesses may see it as desirable to have all employees with perfect command of the English language, imposing such a requirement is potentially discriminatory. The most obvious risk is that of indirect race discrimination as the provision, criteria or practice (PCP) disadvantages those whose mother tongue is not English, and will therefore only be defensible if the employer is able to show objective justification (and that it is proportionate means of achieving a legitimate aim).

In practice, this is likely to mean that, so long as an employee's command of the language is sufficient for them to carry out their duties, an obligation on such employees to have a greater or better command of the language (absent any other good reason) is potentially discriminatory. This means that different roles can have differing language requirements, and one would expect, for example, customer-facing roles such as working on reception to have a higher requirement than roles which require minimal interaction in English, for example, cleaning roles.

Disciplinary action or performance management will clearly not be appropriate in circumstances where the employee does not meet the more demanding language requirements of the employer but has sufficient grasp of the language to carry out the role. Any such action taken could amount to a detriment.

Potential problems

Employers considering exercising a degree of control over language in the workplace should bear in mind the following:

In 2010, an employment tribunal found that an instruction to a Polish worker not to speak Polish at work was direct race discrimination (*Dziedziak v Future Electronics Ltd*)

In 2015, the Employment Appeal Tribunal agreed that an instruction to only speak a particular language in the workplace could be discriminatory (although on the facts of the case, *Kelly v Covance Laboratories Ltd*, it was held not to be because the employer's instruction was based on a genuine concern that the employee may have been an animal rights activist)

The Equality and Human Rights Commission Employment Code of Practice states: "Employers should make sure that any requirement involving the use of a particular language during or outside working hours, for example during work breaks, does not amount to unlawful discrimination"

The Default Retirement Age

The Default Retirement Age (DRA) was phased out between 6th April and 1st October 2011. The change gives people the freedom to continue working for longer. Employers, in the past, (and until 30th September 2011) could make staff retire at 65 even if they were fit and healthy enough to do the job. This could be achieved by giving six months notice to the employee. The last day employees could be retired using the DRA was 30th March 2011. Employers could still use the DRA between 30th March and 6th April, but had to use the 'short notice provisions'. Under these an employee could claim compensation (subject to a maximum of eight weeks wages)

Between 6th April and 30th September, only people who were notified before 6th April 2011, and whose retirement date is before 1st October, could be compulsorily retired. From 1st October, employers could not be able use the DRA to compulsorily retire employees.

There will still be exceptions to these new rules, however. Employers may continue to have a compulsory retirement age, but must be able to prove it is justified at an employment tribunal.

****

Chapter 2

The Role of ACAS

The role of ACAS

ACAS, otherwise known as the Advisory, Conciliation and Arbitration Service, is a Crown non-departmental public body of the United Kingdom's Government. It serves the purpose of improving work-life across organisations by promoting and facilitating strong industrial relations practice.

ACAS strives to achieve this through various media like arbitration and mediation. Above all, ACAS serves to provide collective conciliation function, which helps to resolve disputes between groups of employees or workers (often represented by a trade union) and their employers.

While, ACAS help the involved parties to reach suitable resolutions in case of a dispute, overall, it is an independent and impartial body that does not side with any particular party.

Introduced to further strengthen the Employment Protection Act 1975, ACAS became a household name during the late 1970s and mid-80s when large-scale industrial disputes were quite common. With time, its emphasis has shifted towards aiding businesses to prevent problems especially related to their workforce.

Furthermore, ACAS helps address individual complaints (wherein individuals complain against their employers regarding wrongful dismissal or any other issue) and provide the groundwork for making an employment tribunal claim.

THE ACAS CODE OF PRACTICE

The ACAS Code of Practice on disciplinary and grievance procedures provides the primary practical guidelines to employees, their representatives, and employers, and lays down the groundwork for handling workplace-related issues and disputes.

While the Code is not legally enforceable and non-compliance to it doesn't make an organisation or individual liable to legal proceedings, the employment tribunal will take the Code into account when dealing with relevant cases.

Furthermore, the Code does not apply to dismissals due to non-renewal of fixed-term contracts and redundancy.

The ACAS Code of Practice is issued under the section 199 of the Trade Union and Labour Relations (Consolidation) Act 1992 and was presented before the two Houses of Parliament on 16th January 2015.

The Code that is currently in use, came into effect on 11th March 2015 by the orders of the Secretary of State and has replaced the version issued in 2009.

The ACAS Guide 'Handling small-scale redundancies – a step-by-step guide' and its advisory booklet 'How to manage large-scale redundancies' contain practical guidelines on handling redundancies.

Any failure to abide by the Code does not, in itself, make an employer or organisation liable to legal proceedings. However, it holds relevance in front of an employment tribunal, which may take it into account when considering relevant claims and use to adjust the awarded compensation by up to 25 percent in case of unreasonable failure to comply with the Code's provisions.

This implies that if the employment tribunal finds that an employer has deliberately or unreasonably failed to follow the Code while investigating cases of gross misconduct or any such issues, they hold the jurisdiction to increase any award by as much as 25 percent.

On the other hand, if the tribunal feel that an employee has been unreasonable in making the claim against wrongful dismissal, or failed to follow the guidance provided in the Code, the award may be reduced by up to 25 percent.

KEY POINTS IN THE ACAS CODE OF PRACTICE 2015

First and foremost, the ACAS Code of Practice helps informally resolve a number of potential disciplinary and grievance issues related to a workplace. Cases of one-off incidents of misconduct or unsatisfactory performance are usually dealt in an informal manner with the help of the Code.Having said this, Employment Tribunals in the UK are legally bound to consider the ACAS Code into account when dealing with claims. This, in turn, helps the tribunals to adjust any awards by up to 25 percent for an unreasonable failure to comply with the provisions set out in the code.

In case, there arises a need to take some formal action, the tribunal chooses the action, which is reasonable or justified according to the circumstances of the particular case and the ACAS Code. Subsequently, the Employers are required to deal with the issues promptly, consistently and fairly by conducting investigations to gather and establish relevant facts of the case.

The revised Code of Practice became effective on 11 March 2015 and contains revisions specifically related to the right of accompaniment at grievance and disciplinary hearings. No other section of the Code has been revised. Below are some key points of the Revised Code:

KEY POINTS

1. Disciplinary situations can include misconduct and/or poor performance. The employers may choose to have a separate

capability procedure if they wish to address an employee's performance issues. If so, however, they still need to follow the basic principles of fairness as laid down in the Code (although some adaptations are permitted in this case).

2. Grievances can be concerns, complaints or problems that employees raise with their employers. However, the Code does not apply to the non-renewal of fixed-term contracts once they expire and redundancy dismissals.

The Code promotes transparency and fairness through the development and usage of rules and procedures to handle grievance and disciplinary situations. These procedures should be set down in writing and be specific. Furthermore, both employees and their representatives (where appropriate) must be involved while developing the rules.

In cases, wherein a formal action is required, the employment tribunal will decide the appropriate course after taking into account the resources and size of the employer. This is done because it may not be practicable for all employers to undertake all of the steps set out in the Code, and the onus lies with the tribunal to make sure that a reasonable and justified grievance redressal mechanism was employed.

****

Chapter 3

Contracts of Employment

In the last chapter we looked at employment law generally. In this chapter, we will look more specifically at employment contracts. At the end of the chapter, we will discuss developments in the 'GIG' economy and what this means in terms of contracts of employment. In chapters 3 and 4 we will look specifically at terms of contracts and also implied duties within contract of employment.

When you commence work you may not be given an employment contract. The terms and conditions of your employment may be contained within a staff handbook. However, two months after employment commences you are entitled to a written statement of particulars of employment described below. This will set out the following:

- Your name and the name of your employer
- The date when your employment started
- Your rate of pay, when you will be paid and how the pay has been calculated. This must be at least the minimum wage. Sick pay entitlement should also be included.
- Title of job
- Where job is based
- Your hours of work and holiday entitlement including public holidays. Both of these must provide the maximum/minimum under the Working Time Regulations.
- The title and description of your job and hours of work
- Your notice period

- The employers disciplinary and grievance procedure. (Whilst this was compulsory it is now optional)
- Whether you can join the employers occupational pension scheme if there is one.

You must also be informed in the statement whether the employment is permanent or fixed term. A fixed term contract will state when the employment comes to an end. However, the required notice is still due from the employer. Under the law, if a person has a fixed term contract, the employer must not treat the fixed term employee less favourably than the permanent employee.

A contract of employment will use the terms 'employee' or 'servant' which distinguishes it from a contract of services under which an independent contractor performs services under contract for another person. Legally, the contractor is self-employed and the distinction between an employee and independent contractor is significant. Many Acts of Parliament and statutory regulations demand such a distinction. For example, part V1 of the Employment Protection (consolidation) Act 1978 (now 1996 Employment Rights Act) extends only to persons who are employees. Furthermore, the system of taxation is different as between self-employed and employed persons.

In addition, the concept of vicarious liability normally extends only to the employer/employee relationship. Vicarious liability means that an employer is responsible for the legal consequences of acts done by his employees during the course of work. There are also certain implied terms, such as rights duties and obligations which are implied into every contract of employment, but they do not extend to self employed.

The question of whether the relationship of employer/employee exists is a matter for determination by the courts rather than relying solely on the description or label attached to the contract by the parties. In the case of Young and Woods v. West (1980): the Court of Appeal stated that whether a person is to be regarded as self employed or employed is a question of law not fact. The label which the parties attach to the relationship may be relevant to determining that relationship but it is not conclusive. The courts have developed several tests for distinguishing between employees and contractors.

The tests are as follows:

a. The control test. This test was formulated in the case of Yewens v Noakes (1880). Bramwell J stated " A servant is a person subject to the command of his master as to the manner in which he shall do his work" Does the person alleged to be the employer actually control the employee in respect of the work done and the performance of that work. If the answer was in the affirmative the relationship of employer/employee was established. In practice this test is largely redundant as working practices and societal norms have changed over the years.

b. The integration test. This test was first stated in precise terms by Denning LJ in Stevenson, Jordan and Harrison v. Macdonald and Evans (1952):

'One feature which seems to run through the instances is that, under a contract of service, a man is employed as part of the business, and his work is done as an integral part of the business: whereas, under a contract for services, his work, although done for the business, is not integrated into it, but is only accessory to it'

c. The economic reality test. In recent years the courts have used a more flexible approach which incorporates both of the previous tests. This is referred to as the economic reality test and means that factors such as control, integration and powers of selection etc are simply issues which contribute to the decision which must be based

47

on all the circumstances. Held: there are three conditions which establish a contract of service:

a. The employee agrees to provide his own work and skill
b. There must be some element of control exercisable by the employer: and
c. The other terms of the contract must not be inconsistent with a contract of service.

In this case, a consideration of point (c) and particularly the question of the use of substitute drivers led to the finding that the driver was an independent contractor.

Recently, the tribunals and courts have tended to ask the single fundamental question: 'is the person who has engaged himself to perform these services performing them as a person in business on his own account'. Young and Woods V West (1980) is an important case in this respect. West worked for the appellants as a sheet metal worker, however choosing to pay his own tax and National Insurance. He had no entitlement to holiday or sick pay. Following the termination of his contract he claimed to be an employee and pursued a claim for unfair dismissal.

The Court of Appeal, applying the above test, said that it was impossible to regard West as being in business on his own account. Apart from handling his own deductions, and having no holiday or sick pay, West's conditions were the same as other workers. One of the many problems arising out of the distinction between an employee and an independent contractor is that, particularly in the construction industry, workers are often taken on on the basis that they are self-employed, although, to all intents and purposes, they may appear employed. This is called the "lump" which means that the person contracting his services is paid a lump sum payment and takes care of his own tax, national insurance etc. The employer is absolved of responsibility for PAYE etc. Since 1971, legislative

48

provisions have existed whose purpose is to minimise the income tax evasion through use of a system of exempting certificates available only to genuine sub- contractors. The most recent of these provisions are those contained in the Finance Act 1979.

Selection of employees

A number of statutory restrictions have been introduced which affect the employer's right to employ who he chooses. The main ones are the Disability Discrimination Act 1996, now replaced by the Equality Act 2010, The Rehabilitation of Offenders Act 1974, the Sex Discrimination Act 1975 now replaced by the Equality Act 2010 and the Race Relations Act 1976 now replaced by the Equality Act 2010.

Rehabilitation of Offenders Act 1974 (as amended)

The 1974 Act, as amended in 2014, allows a person to 'live down' certain convictions after a specified period of between six months and ten years, depending on the conviction and sentence, a conviction is deemed to be spent providing no serious offence has been committed during the rehabilitation period. The Act provides that normally a spent conviction or failure to disclose it, is no ground for refusing to employ or dismiss a person or discriminate against him in employment. It should be noted that regulations under the Act means that it does not apply to a number of kinds of employment including teaching, medicine, accountancy etc.

Continuous employment

The concept of 'continuous employment is very important in that nearly all of the various statutory rights afforded employees are dependent upon the acquisition by the employee of two years continuous employment, as a minimum. The rules for computing the period of continuous employment are contained in schedule 13 of the Employment Rights (Consolidation) Act 1996.

Employment is presumed to be continuous unless the contrary is shown. Any week in which the employee is employed for sixteen hours or more counts towards computing the period of employment. These do not include 'hours on call'. Sickness injury etc does not discount weeks.

One vital question is: can separate concurrent contracts, with the same employer, be aggregated in order to give a person continuity of employment? In Lewis v. Surrey County Council (1987) L had worked for the council since 1969 in three art colleges. L had separate contracts for each college term and for each of the three courses. Each contract was confined to the particular department concerned. The contract merely specified the total number of hours to be worked. The House of Lords held that the contracts could not be aggregated as the legislation referred to only one single contractual obligation. The House of Lords did however indicate that L should have pleaded that the three contracts amounted to one single contract. Any week in which an employee is absent on account of a 'temporary cessation' of work counts in the calculation of a period of continuous employment. Any week during which an employee is absent counts towards continuous employment if, by arrangement or custom, the employment is regarded as continuous. Any week in which an employee is on strike, or absent from work because of a lock out, does not count in computing the period of employment but does not break continuity.

If an employee is employed for more than 16 hours per week and then becomes employed for less than 16 hours but more than 8 hours, he will, for a further period of twenty-six weeks, be treated as employed for more than 16 hours per week. If an employee has been employed for more than 8 hours per week, but less than 16, and has been so employed for five years, he is regarded as being continuously employed for that period.

Transfer of undertakings

There are various provisions dealing with the question of continuity of employment for the purposes of employment protection rights. The 1978 Act Schedule 13 and the Transfer of Undertakings (Protection of Employment) Regulations 1981 (TUPE) deal with these. The net effect of the provisions is that where there is a transfer to a new employer, continuity is not broken. There have been a few changes as a result of new regulations in 2013, see chapter on redundancy.

Specific employment contracts

Some groups of employees are in a special position with regard to contracts of employment.

The below lists the main groups.

Directors and partners

A company director is regarded as an employee for most of the statutory purposes if he has a written service contract with the company, but a non-executive director is not usually regarded as an employee. Whether such a service contract exists is a matter of law, to be determined by reference to the facts of the particular case. Thus, even the director of a one-man business may be an employee. One important case dealing with the employment rights of directors is that of Eaton v. Robert Eaton and Secretary of State for Employment (1988). Eaton was the managing director of RE Ltd. When the company ceased trading, he applied to the tribunal for a redundancy payment. No payment was granted as there was nothing in writing to indicate that E was an employee of the company and since 1981 E had not received any financial remuneration from the company because of its financial position. The EAT supported the decision of the tribunal as they could not find fault with the finding that E was a 'office holder' and therefore not an employee.

Partners

A partner in a firm is self-employed. If a person is employed by partners, the relationship of employer/employee exists.

Apprentices

Apprentices working under contracts of apprenticeship are regarded as employees with all the relevant employment law rights. A key feature of contracts of apprenticeship is that training is regarded as the primary purpose of the arrangement with the work performed by the apprentice being regarded as secondary. It is critical that employers appreciate and understand this since this is the reason why apprentices employed under a contract of apprenticeship have enhanced rights on termination meaning that employers owe them greater obligations.

In Wallace v CA Roofing Services, Mr Wallace was taken on as an apprentice. There was no written contract of apprenticeship, but his written terms and conditions stated that he was an "apprentice sheet metal worker" and included a provision that "at the end of your apprenticeship your employment will terminate unless there is a suitable vacancy that we can offer you at the time". The period of the agreement was four years, but his written terms included a recital of the statutory minimum notice periods.

After 19 months, Mr Wallace was dismissed as redundant because of a fall off in work. He argued that his contract was a contract of apprenticeship and therefore could not be terminated for that reason. The high court held that the agreement under which he was employed was a contract of apprenticeship, rather than a contract of employment or a training contract. The court noted that although modern legislation had assimilated apprenticeships to contracts of employment, the contract of apprenticeship still remained a distinct entity at common law. Its primary purpose is training and the execution of work for the employer is secondary.

Termination of a contract of apprenticeship

As discussed above the primary focus of a contract of apprenticeship is on training; consequently an employer cannot dismiss an apprentice working under a contract of apprenticeship on the same grounds that they can dismiss an ordinary employee.

Poor performance

In Dunk v George Waller & Sons [1970] 2 all ER 630, the court of appeal held that apprentices are entitled to damages for loss of earnings and training for the remainder of the term and for loss of future career prospects. Mr Dunk entered into a four-year apprenticeship. For the first couple of years, he worked reasonably well and progressed through the business. However, he struggled with the exams, and when he failed a particular exam, his employer considered he was unlikely to pass a second time and terminated his apprenticeship. He sought damages for breach.

The court of appeal stated:

"*an apprenticeship agreement is of a special character... he is entitled to damages for his loss of earnings and of training during the remainder of the term of apprenticeship agreement and also for the diminution of his future prospects.*"

The damages that employers can be required to pay can therefore be significant, taking into account the remainder of the term of the apprenticeship, as well as loss of training and impact on future earnings.

Misconduct

An employer has less scope for dismissing an apprentice employed under a contract of apprenticeship than an ordinary employee. Misconduct in the normal employment context will not usually be sufficient, unless the apprentice's actions are so extreme that the apprentice is effectively un-trainable.

Redundancy

Apprentices employed under a contract of apprenticeship cannot be dismissed by reason of redundancy in the usual way, unless there is a closure of the business or the employer's business undergoes a fundamental change in its character.

Apprenticeship agreements

Apprenticeship agreements were introduced under the apprenticeships, skills, children and learning act 2009 (ASCLA 2009). The ASCLA 2009 introduced the new concept of an apprenticeship agreement. The key development for employers to understand is that an apprenticeship agreement is separate and distinct from the more traditional contract of apprenticeship. The distinction is extremely important, since as we have seen above apprentices working under contracts of apprenticeship have greater rights than ordinary employees (which includes employees who are employed under an apprenticeship agreement).

The following four conditions are required for an agreement to qualify as an apprenticeship agreement:

- The apprentice must undertake to work for the employer;
- The agreement must be in the "prescribed form". The prescribed form is laid down in the apprenticeship agreement regulations, which state that the agreement must contain the basic terms of employment required to be given to employees under section 1 of the era 1996. This can be in the form of a written statement of

particulars of employment, a written contract of employment or a letter of engagement;

* The agreement must also include a statement of the skill, trade or occupation for which the apprentice is being trained under the relevant apprenticeship framework;
* The agreement must state that it is governed by the law of England and Wales; and

The agreement must state that it is entered into in connection with a qualifying apprenticeship framework (information on what constitutes an apprenticeship framework can be found at http://www.afo.sscalliance.org/).

Termination of an apprenticeship agreement

If the apprentice is employed under an apprenticeship agreement, then it is deemed a contract of service and the normal principles for breach of contract and unfair dismissal claims apply. This means that employers can manage under-performing apprentices and deal with disciplinary issues as they would with any other employee in the business.

Public sector employees

In the case of Crown servants, a relationship is enjoyed between Crown and employee which is analogous to a contract of employment, subject to an implied right of the Crown to dismiss without notice. Employees of nationalised industries and local authorities are not Crown employees. Unless an Act so provides, it does not bind the Crown. A number of modern employment law provisions, however, have been extended to cover the Crown.

Police

The police are excluded from many of the statutory rights to which other employees are entitled, e.g. the right to present a complaint of unfair dismissal. In addition, the rights of police officers to be members of trade unions and to engage in industrial action are severely limited. However, as 'office holders' police officers cannot be dismissed without a hearing and have a right to reinstatement in the event of the dismissal being found to be wrongful.

The armed forces

The armed forces are excluded from the various statutory rights enjoyed by employees. One of the questions which has been recently raised is whether or not a public sector employee is able to have the decision of his/her dismissal reviewed by the court through the judicial review procedure.

As the normal route of Industrial Tribunal cannot be followed by a 'office holder' e.g. a police officer, judicial review is appropriate to obtain a remedy as there is no alternative. The mere existence of a contract however will not stop a court from reviewing a decision where it thinks appropriate. One important case is McGoldrick v. London Borough of Brent (1987).

Minors

The ordinary rule of the law of contract is to the effect that a minor (person under eighteen) is bound by a contract of employment if the agreement as a whole is substantially to that persons benefit. In Doyle v. White City Stadium LTD and the British Boxing Board of Control (1935) an infant boxer held a BBBC license to box. After one contest he was disqualified and in accordance with BBBC rules his purse with- held. He claimed that the contract was not binding on him so the purse could not be withheld. The courts held that the contract was substantially to his benefit so the BBBC was within its rights to withhold the purse. In addition to common law there are some statutory restrictions covering minors.

The Children and Young Persons Act 1933 and the Employment of Children Act 1973 regulate the employment of those minors below school leaving age (16). These Acts prevent the employment of any person under 13. Between the ages of 13-16 a minor may be employed in part time work subject to the restrictions as to the number of hours which may be worked and as to the time of such work.

There are also restrictions as to the employment in certain jobs, e.g. factories and mines. Between the ages of 16 and 18, minors are classed as young persons and in various legislative provisions restrictions are imposed upon the kind of work and the number of hours which such persons may do. The Sex Discrimination Act 1986, now replaced by the Equality Act 2010, removed most of the existing statutory provisions restricting women's hours of work.

In addition to the Acts mentioned, the below is a summary of legislation which has a bearing on the employment of minors.

Apart from local authority byelaws the main Acts and regulations which govern employment of children are:
• The Children and Young Persons Act 1933 Part II and section 107, amended by the Children (Protection at Work) Regulations 1998 (S.I. 1998/276),the Children (Protection at Work) Regulations 2000 (S.I. 2000/1333) and the Children (Protection at Work) (No 2) Regulations 2000 (S.I.2000/2548).
• Children and Young Persons Act 1963 section 35(2).
• The Criminal Justice and Court Services Act 2000 Part II.
• The Education Act 1996, sections 558 to 560. • The Employment of Women, Young Persons and Children Act 1920.
•The Gambling Act 2005, sections 51 to 55. • The House to House Collections Regulations 1947 (SR&O 1947/2662) amended by the House to House Collections Regulations 1963 (S.I. 1963/684), regulation 8.

• The Licensing Act 2003, sections 145 and 153.

• The Merchant Shipping Act 1995 section 55. See also Merchant Shipping Notice MSN 1776(M).

• The Riding Establishments Act 1964, amended by the Riding Establishments Act 1970, section 1(4A).

•The Safeguarding Vulnerable Groups Act 2006.

• The Management of Health and Safety at Work Regulations 1999 (S.I. 1999/3242) amended by the Management of Health and Safety at Work and Fire Precautions (Workplace) (Amendment) Regulations 2003 (S.I. 2003/2457).

• The Working Time Regulations 1998 (S.I.1998/1833).

Temporary employees

Once an employee has completed the appropriate period for continuous employment (notably one year for unfair dismissal) he is eligible to claim the various statutory rights. An employee who is engaged expressly as a temporary employee to replace someone suspended on medical grounds or absent on maternity leave is not normally regarded as unfairly dismissed when the absent employee returns.

Probationary employees

An employee may be engaged subject to a probationary period, the employer retaining the right to terminate or confirm the contract within or at the end of the specified time. Once the employee has completed the stated time he is eligible to present a complaint of unfair dismissal. As with any other dismissal, which is alleged to be unfair, the employer must show that he acted reasonably. Regular appraisals are seen as necessary evidence by tribunals in order to demonstrate that the employee under probation knew he may be dismissed.

Employees on fixed term contracts

Under such contracts employment rights depend on whether the contracts can be aggregated in order to give the employee continuous employment. There is no statutory definition of fixed term contract. However, following the decision in BBC v. Dixon (1979) it is clear that a fixed term contract is not fixed if it contains a clause for early termination.

A fixed term contract is one which expires on a particular date, rather than on the performance of a task or the happening of an event.

Fixed Term Working Regulations

The 2002 Employment Act implemented the long-awaited Fixed Term Employees (Prevention of less Favorable Treatment) Regulations which came into force on 1st October 2002. The Regulations were prompted by the need to ensure that British law complies with the EC Fixed Term Work Directives 1999/70/EC. In summary, the following are covered:

- Casual workers
- Seasonal workers
- Those on short term contracts
- Those employed for a specific task or project
- Those on temporary cover contracts
- Those on zero-hour contracts

A contract for a fixed period of time automatically terminates at the end of the period.

If the employment is for less than four weeks there is no entitlement, as of right, to a statement giving the main terms of employment or to any period of notice terminating the employment.

If the fixed term is for one year or more and is not renewed then the employee is treated as having been dismissed and a claim for unfair dismissal might arise, If the fixed term is for two years or more and not renewed then a claim for unfair dismissal might arise.

In essence fixed term workers cannot be treated less favorably than their colleagues who are permanent employees unless there is an objective reason for doing so. Any intention to use fixed term contracts as a method of avoiding employment legislation will be carefully scrutinized by Employment Tribunals. Such a purpose is against the spirit of the legislation.

Persons over retiring age

The law in this area has recently been changed because of the European Court of Justice decision in Marshall v. Southampton and South West Hampshire Area Health Authority. (1986) This decision meant that the equal treatment directive was directly applicable to state employees, but legislation was required to provide a remedy for private sector employees. The decision concerned men and women being required to retire at different ages which the ECJ held to be discriminatory. The response of the Government was to pass the Sex Discrimination Act 1986 which gave effect to the decision in Marshall but also made other amendments.

Zero Hours Contracts

Recent figures from the Office for National Statistics have shown that the total number of people working on zero hours contracts increased from 1.7million in 2016 to 1.8million in 2017. Trade unions have asked for this kind of contract to be banned, claiming they allow companies to exploit people, and the government has shown concern as to their use.

What is a zero hours contract?

A zero hours contract is one where a person is not contracted to work a set number of hours, and is only paid for the number of hours actually worked. These individuals are often classed as 'workers', not 'employees'.

What's the difference between a 'worker' and an 'employee'?

There is no comprehensive legal definition of 'worker' or 'employee' and this has created difficulties. Due to this ambiguity, employment tribunals have developed certain tests to define the difference. One of the main defining factors is 'mutuality of obligations'. In a nutshell, if you are a worker, your employer doesn't have to offer you work and you don't have to accept, hence there is no 'mutuality of obligations'. This is because it is often a very casual, ad-hoc relationship. This is different to being an employee who is contracted for a certain amount of hours per week and is expected to work those hours.

Does a worker on a zero hour contract have less rights than an employee?

Workers have considerably less rights. As an example, they cannot bring an unfair dismissal claim or claim a statutory redundancy payment. Workers do, however, have statutory rights - for example, paid annual leave under the working time regulations, the national minimum wage, and protection from discrimination. There is often a blurred line on whether an individual is a 'worker' or an 'employee'. Whenever there is a dispute about a person's employment status, the tribunal will scrutinise the nature of the working arrangements. Even if an individual has a zero hours contract, this will have no weighting if it does not truly reflect the actual working relationship.

Trade unions claim that companies use zero hours contracts to avoid agency working regulations and the rights that employees have. Trying to juggle family life with no certain income and arranging childcare is difficult when a person doesn't know when or if they will be working. The main concern is not the lack of work offered to those on zero hours contracts (figures shows that only 14% on zero hour contracts complain that they are not offered regular hours), but the fact that in some cases employers will engage someone on a zero hour contact when in reality it is a misrepresentation of the actual working relationship, with many people not getting the rights they truly deserve as employees.

On 26 May 2015, new regulations about zero hours contracts were brought in. The law prevents employers from enforcing 'exclusivity clauses' in a zero hours contract. An exclusivity clause would be where an employer restricts workers from working for other employers.

Trade unions are being very vocal in saying that they want these type of contracts to be banned, and lawyers for many years have wanted clear statutory definitions for 'employee' and 'worker' under law.

The 'gig' economy

What is the so-called "gig" economy, a phrase increasingly in use, and seemingly so in connection with employment disputes? According to one definition, it is "a labour market characterised by the prevalence of short-term contracts or freelance work, as opposed to permanent jobs". And - taking opposing partisan viewpoints - it is either a working environment that offers flexibility with regard to employment hours, or... it is a form of exploitation with very little workplace protection.

Flexibility

In the gig economy, instead of a regular wage, workers get paid for the "gigs" they do, such as a food delivery or a car journey. In the UK it's estimated that five million people are employed in this type of capacity. Jobs include couriers, ride-hailing drivers and video producers.

Proponents of the gig economy claim that people can benefit from flexible hours, with control over how much time they can work as they juggle other priorities in their lives. In addition, the flexible nature often offers benefits to employers, as they only pay when the work is available, and don't incur staff costs when the demand is not there.

Meanwhile, workers in the gig economy are classed as independent contractors. That means they have no protection against unfair dismissal, no right to redundancy payments, and no right to receive the national minimum wage, paid holiday or sickness pay. It is these aspects that are proving contentious.

The latest attempt to bring a degree of legal clarity to the employment status of people in the gig economy has been playing out in the Court of Appeal. A London firm, Pimlico Plumbers, lost its appeal against a previous ruling that said one of its long-serving plumbers was a worker - entitled to basic rights, including holiday pay - rather than an independent contractor.

Like other cases of a similar nature, all cases found that these employers were 'disguising' workers who are in reality entitled to basic rights such as annual leave and the National Minimum and National Living wage.

In the past few year two tribunal hearings have gone against employers looking to classify staff as independent contractors.

In October 2016 two Uber drivers won a case to be classed as workers rather than independent contractors. The ruling by a

London employment tribunal meant drivers for the ride-hailing app would be entitled to holiday pay, paid rest breaks and the national minimum wage. The GMB union described the decision as a "monumental victory" for some 40,000 drivers in England and Wales. In December, Uber launched an appeal against the ruling that it had acted unlawfully (Aslam and Others v Uber BV and others (EAT October 2016). The appeal was heard in october 2018 and is on hold. In June 2018, 65 couriers won their fight against Hermes Delivery Services to be recognised as workers.

And in January this year, **a** tribunal found that Maggie Dewhurst, a courier with logistics firm City Sprint, should be classed as a worker rather than independent contractor, entitling her to basic rights.

'New ways of working'

One difference worth noting is that workers in the gig economy differ slightly from those on zero-hours contracts. Like workers in the gig economy, zero-hours contractors - or casual contractors - don't get guaranteed hours or much job security from their employer.

But people on zero-hours contracts are seen as employees in some sense, as they are entitled to holiday pay. But, like those in the gig economy, they are not entitled to sick pay. Meanwhile, the Department for Business is holding an inquiry into a range of working practices - including the gig economy. The department says it wants to ensure its employment rules are up to date to reflect "new ways of working".

****

Chapter 4

Employment Contracts-Terms of Contract

Significance of the terms of contract

In any dispute between an employer and employee, the terms of the contract are of considerable significance in that one party may have a right to take legal action against the other in respect of any breach of contract. Of more importance is the significance of the terms of contract when an action for unfair dismissal is brought.

In such a case, although the question of whether one or more parties has broken the contract is of considerable importance, other considerations arise-notably whether the employer acted reasonably in dismissing the employee. Prior to the introduction of the remedy of unfair dismissal, an employer could always terminate the contract provided that he gave proper notice. The employee would have no recourse in law.

Sources of the terms of the contract

The terms of the contract of employment may be derived from a number of sources: minimum statutory standards; express statements of the parties; collective agreements; works rules books; custom; duties of employees; duties of employers.

It should be noted that, by virtue of the 1996 Employment Rights Act, an employer is under an obligation to supply his employees with a written statement containing information as to certain terms of the contract of employment.

65

Minimum Statutory Standards

In effect all those statutory rights and duties which apply to the employer/employee relationship may be said to form part of every contract of employment except those to which the statutory provisions do not apply. With very few exceptions it is not possible for parties to contract out of statutory provisions.

Minimum terms orders

Certain bodies, notably wage councils, are empowered to make orders which take effect as part of individual contracts of employment and are enforceable as such. It should be noted that the powers of wage councils were limited by the Wages Act 1986, itself consolidated by the 1996 Employment Rights Act.

Express statements of the parties

Nature of express statements. An express statement, in this context, is a statement, either oral or written, made by the employer to the employee (or vice versa) concerning the terms of the contract. Such statements may include letters of appointment, formal contracts drawn up by the employer, verbal statements as to the terms and conditions of employment upon which the person is to be employed (as to wages hours holidays etc) or other statements. If an express statement is made before the parties enter into the contract of employment, it forms part of the contract and may not be subsequently altered without the mutual consent of the parties. If one party deviates from the agreed pre-contractual terms, that party is in breach of contract unless the other consents to the deviation either expressly or by deviation.

Post-contractual statements. Post-contractual statements do not form part of the contract of employment unless the parties expressly or implicitly agree that such a statement does become part of the contract. If an employee is employed upon certain terms which are not stated prior to the commencement of the contract and he is subsequently given a written statement which differs from the original terms the written statement does not supersede the written terms because the written statement is not to be regarded as contractual but merely as evidence of the contract.

Collective agreements

The term 'collective agreement' has a particular definition in s 178 (1) of the Trade Unions and Labour Relations (consolidation) Act 1992 but in general terms it may be described as an agreement between a trade union and an employer or employers association which deals, amongst other things, with the terms and conditions of employment of employees of the employer who is a party to the agreement. A collective agreement must be considered at two levels:

a) its effect as between the parties to it;
b) Its effect upon the individual contract of employment of the employees who are the object of the agreement.

It has been estimated that 75% of all employees have their terms and conditions of employment determined by collective agreements and it is therefore important to know the extent to which as a matter of law, such agreements form part of the individual contract of employment. This is sometimes referred to as the 'normative' effect of collective agreements. Several arguments have been advanced to suggest that a collective agreement must automatically be regarded as forming part of the contracts of employment of those employees to whom the agreement refers; but these arguments have generally been refuted by the courts.

The correctness of this view has been put under pressure by the

67

Court of Appeal decision in Marley v Forward Trust Group Ltd (1986). M was employed as a field supervisor in F's Bristol office. His terms and conditions of employment incorporated the terms of a collective agreement with ASTMS, and included both a mobility and redundancy clause, the latter allowing a six-month trial period. However, the final clause of the agreement stated that the agreement is binding in honour only.

F closed their Bristol office and M worked in London, under the terms of the agreement, for a trial period. He found the job unsuitable and sought a redundancy payment. Both the IT and the EAT rejected his claim on the ground that the agreement was stated to be binding in honour only and was, accordingly, unenforceable. The Court of Appeal rejected this and held that the terms of an unenforceable collective agreement can be incorporated into contract so of employment and are then enforceable against the individual employee. The unenforceable nature of the agreement was limited to the parties to the agreement, in this case the employer and the union.

Express incorporation. It is fairly well established that it is possible to incorporate a collective agreement into an individual contract of employment if the contract expressly provides that this is to be the case. In National Coal Board v Galley (1958) it was held that a clause of a collective agreement which stated that colliery deputies would work 'such days or part days in each week as may reasonably be required by the employer' could be regarded as being part of the original contracts of employment because the contracts of the deputies referred to that collective agreement as being the source of the terms of the contracts.

It should be noted that the written statement supplied pursuant to the 1992 Act permits the employer to refer an employee to a document, such as a collective agreement, as being the source of certain terms of the contract of employment. A Collective

68

agreement may also expressly become part of a contract of employment by virtue of statutory provisions. There are a number of situations where this is possible:

a) under the 1992 Act. Provision is made for application to be made to the Secretary of State for the approval of dismissals procedures agreements. Such agreements, which replace the right to claim unfair dismissal for those employees covered, form part of the terms of employment of those employees within their ambit;

b) under the 1992 Act, a collective agreement may be made which substitutes for the right to claim a redundancy payment under the provisions of the 1996 Act, a right to claim under the collective agreement If such an agreement approved by the Secretary of State, it forms part of the terms of employment of those employees to whom it applies;

c) under the 1992 Act a collective agreement may be made which substitutes for the right to a guarantee payment under the provisions of the 1996 Act, a right to claim under the collective agreement. It should be noted that where the terms of a collective agreement are expressly incorporated and varied by consent between the unions and employers the new terms become incorporated into the individual contracts of employment; however, unilateral variation or abrogation of the agreement by one party does not have a corresponding effect on individual employment contracts (Robertson A and Jackson v British Gas (1983).

Works rule-books

A works rulebook can take a number of forms in so far as it may consist of an actual book given to each employee when he enters employment or at some subsequent date. These rules relate to disciplinary action, suspension, dismissal for conduct etc. Safety procedures are normally incorporated. S.3 of the Employment

Rights Act 1996 states that an employer must give details of disciplinary and grievance procedures to an employee when taking up employment.

As far as the effect on contract goes, if the employer gives the employee the rulebook, or expressly refers to it before a contract is signed then it is considered to be part of the contract. In Petrie v Macfisheries (1940) a notice was posted on the wall of the work place stating the circumstances in which sick pay would be paid. The plaintiff claimed that it was not part of his contract. The defendant's case was upheld as the rule concerning sick pay was deemed to be incorporated into his contract as a result of his continued working at the place.

Not all works rules will be part of the contract, particularly where there are numerous rules contained in the relevant documentation, some for example may be out of date and inappropriate. This is well illustrated by the decision in Secretary of State for Employment v ASLEF (1972) a case concerning the rule book of British Rail, where Lord Denning said ' Each man signs a form saying that he will abide by the rules but these rules are in no way terms of the contract of employment. They are only instructions to a man as to how to do his work'.

Custom

Custom plays a significant part in employment law. It seems that there are four different categories of custom, which may form part of a contract of employment.

a) Custom of a particular place of work.

b) Custom of an industry or trade.

c) Custom of a specific geographical locality.

d) Customary conduct of the parties to the contract of employment.

a) See Marshall v English Electric !1945)

b) See Sagar v Ridehalgh (1931) and Davson v France (1959)

c) Sagar v Ridehalgh

d) Mears v Safecar Security (1982)

****

Chapter 5

Employment Contracts-Implied Duties of the Employer/Employee

Into every contract of employment are implied a number of obligations in so far as these are not inconsistent with the express terms of the individual contract of employment. These duties are based on principles developed by the courts in the decided cases.

Implied duties may be classified as follows:
a) to be ready and willing to work;

b) to use reasonable care and skill;

c) to obey lawful orders;

d) to take care of the employers property;

e) to act in good faith.

To be ready and willing to work
The fundamental duty owed to an employer by an employee is to be turn up to work and to work at the direction of the employer in return for wages. Two interesting cases have arisen in relation to this. In Miles v Wakefield Metropolitan District Council (1987) M was a superintendent registrar of births deaths and marriages, working 37 hours per week, three of which were on Saturday morning. As part of industrial action, M refused to carry out

marriages on Saturday mornings, although he was willing to do his other work. Wages were deducted, M sued for lost wages and the employer won, with the House of Lords (Supreme Court) saying that where an employee refuses to perform the full range of duties and had been told that he would not be paid if he did not, then the employers were entitled to withhold the whole of his remuneration, (3hrs) although he attended for work and carried out a substantial part of his duties.

To use reasonable care and skill

This has two aspects:

a) The duty not to be unduly negligent.

b) The duty to be reasonably competent.

If an employee is negligent during the course of his work, he may be regarded as being in breach of contract. In Lister v Romford Ice and Cold Storage Ltd (1957) a lorry driver, employed by the company, carelessly reversed his lorry and injured a fellow employee, who was his father. The employers paid damages to the father but claimed indemnity from the son, because of negligence. This was held to be the case.

Duty to be reasonably competent

If an employee is incompetent this may be a breach of contract. In Hamer v Cornelius (1858) this was held to be the case.

To obey lawful orders

An employee is under a duty to obey all the lawful orders of his employer, i.e. those which are within the scope of the contract. In Price v Mouat (1862) a lace salesman was ordered to card (pack) lace but he refused and was dismissed without notice. He claimed wrongful dismissal and this was held because the order was not one which was within the scope of his contract.

An employee, therefore, is not obliged to do any act, which is deemed to fall outside the ambit of his individual contract of employment. The question of the introduction of new technology has caused problems here and must be linked to the scope of managerial prerogative in introducing new work techniques. In Cresswell v Board of Inland Revenue (1984) the Revenue wished to introduce a computer system to assist with the PAYE system. The majority of the work associated with the system had been done manually. Did the employers have the ability to change the nature of the working system? Did the employers have the ability to change the nature of the working system? Held: employees were expected to adopt the new methods and techniques in performing their contracts if the employer provided the necessary training in new skills.

To take care of employers property

An employer is under an obligation to take reasonable care of his employer's property. In Superflux v Plaisted (1958) the defendant had been in charge of a team of vacuum cleaner salesmen and had negligently allowed fourteen cleaners to be stolen from his van. Held: he was in breach of his contract of employment.

To act in good faith

His implied duty has several different aspects, which together form the basis of a relationship of trust. There is the duty not to make a secret profit, i.e. not to accept bribes.

This principal was clear from the case of Reading v AG (1951) which concerned a member of the armed forces, in which Lord Normand said:

---though the relation of a member of his majesty's forces is not

74

accurately described as that of a servant under a contract of service--he owes to the Crown a duty as full fiduciary as the duty of a servant to his master--and in consequence--all profits and advantages gained by the use of his military status are to be for the benefit of the Crown'.

Duty to disclose certain information.

There appears to be no general duty on an employee to inform his employer of his misconduct and deficiencies: Bell v Lever Brothers (1932). However, there is one important exception, namely where the employment of that particular person is made more hazardous by virtue of an undisclosed defect on part of the employee.

Covenants in restraint of trade

A covenant in restraint of trade is a clause in a contract, which purports to limit an employees rights to seek employment when and where he chooses upon leaving his employment. This is usually done as a protective measure by an employer when he might suffer as a result of disclosure of confidential information or for other such reasons.

There are difficulties however, in enforcing such covenants and the employer has to demonstrate that the covenant is justified. A court will look at such factors as the time that the covenant runs, geographical area that it covers and public interest when considering the reasonableness of such covenants.

If a covenant is found to be unreasonable, the contract as a whole is not necessarily regarded as void, unless it is impossible to distinguish the covenant from the rest of the contract. If the covenant can be severed from the rest of the contract, without altering the nature of the agreement, the unreasonable clause may be struck out: see Commercial Plastics LTD v Vincent (1965).

If an employer breaks the contract of employment by wrongfully dismissing an employee, the employee may disregard any covenant in the contract which purports to limit his right to seek employment elsewhere: see General Billposting v Atkinson (1909).

Patents

At common law, unless the contract dealt with the matter, an employee would not normally be entitled to the benefit of any invention made by him if to allow him to do so would be a contravention of the implied duty of the employee to act in good faith.

The Patents Act 1977, ss-39-47, gives ownership of an invention to the employee inventor unless the invention was made in the course of the duties for which he was employed. Any disputes are dealt with by the patents court.

Duties of the employer

By virtue of common law, and a number of statutory provisions, employers have a considerable number of obligations towards employees. The main examples are:

To pay contractually agreed remuneration

An employer is under no obligation to provide work as long as remuneration is paid. This however, has been questioned in recent times, particularly in relation to skilled employees. Lord Denning said, in Langston v AUEW (1973): 'In these days an employer, when employing a skilled man, is bound to provide him with work. By which I mean that the man should be given the opportunity of doing his work when it is available and when he is ready and willing to do it'. Therefore, a failure to provide work of a nature that the employee is used to could be regarded as constructive dismissal.

There are three exceptions to the rule, one is piecework, the second is where the nature of the employment is such that the

76

actual performance of the work forms part of the consideration supplied by the employer, the employee may be entitled to compensation over and above the contractual wages. These situations are sometimes referred to as 'names in lights' clauses. the other exception is when an employee is taking part in limited industrial action.

To pay the National Minimum Wage and National Living Wage

The National Minimum Wage (NMW) is the minimum pay per hour most workers in the UK are entitled to by law. The rate varies depending on age and whether a person is an apprentice. Most workers who are 25 or older must be paid at least the National Living Wage (NLW), which is the highest rate of the National Minimum Wage.

National Minimum Wage and National Living Wage Rates for 2018/19

Age	Minimum hourly rate 2018-19	2019-20
25 and over	£7.83	£8.21
21 to 24	£7.38	£7.70
18 to 20	£5.90	£6.15
Under 18	£4.20	£4.35
Apprentice	£3.70	£3.90

Apprentices and the National Minimum Wage

Apprentices are entitled to the apprentice rate of the National Minimum Wage if they are either:

- Under 19
- 19 or over and in the first year of their apprenticeship

Apprentices over 19 who have completed the first year of their apprenticeship are entitled to the National Minimum Wage for their age.

Entitlement to the National Minimum Wage

A person must be at least school leaving age (the last Friday in June of the school year in which the person turns 16) to get the National Minimum Wage. Almost all workers are entitled to the National Minimum Wage, including:

- Casual workers
- Part-time workers
- Temporary workers

There are some types of workers who don't qualify:

- self-employed people running their own business
- company directors
- volunteers or voluntary workers
- workers on a government employment programme, such as the Work Programme
- members of the armed forces
- family members of the employer living in the employer's home

- non-family members living in the employer's home who share in the work and leisure activities, are treated as one of the family and are not charged for meals or accommodation, for example au pairs
- workers younger than school leaving age (usually 16)
- higher and further education students on a work placement up to 1 year
- workers on government pre-apprenticeships schemes
- people on the following European Union programmes: Leonardo da Vinci, Youth in Action, Erasmus, Comenius
- people working on a Jobcentre Plus Work trial for 6 weeks
- share fishermen
- prisoners
- people living and working in a religious community

Work experience and internships

A person will not get the National Minimum Wage or National Living Wage if they are:

- a student doing work experience as part of a higher or further education course
- of compulsory school age
- a volunteer or doing voluntary work
- on a government or European programme
- work shadowing

Voluntary work

A person is classed as doing voluntary work if they can only get certain limited benefits (for example reasonable travel or lunch expenses) and they are working for a:

- charity
- voluntary organisation or associated fund-raising body
- statutory body

How the National Minimum Wage and National Living Wage are calculated

Deductions from your pay before National Minimum Wage is calculated: If an employee has paid for certain things related to their job out of their wages, the employer should deduct these payments before they calculate whether they have been paid the correct minimum wage.

These payments are:
- Payments for the employer's own use or benefit - for example, if they have paid for travel between work sites
- Payments for things needed for the job but aren't refunded for – such as tools, uniform or equipment
- All other payments made out of wages, such as tax and National Insurance, should be included when the employer calculates whether the employee has been paid the National Minimum Wage.

Minimum wage for different types of work – and what counts as working time

The National Minimum Wage is worked out as an hourly rate, but it applies even if the employee is not paid by the hour.

Accommodation and the National Minimum Wage

If an employer provides accommodation, they can take the value of this into account when calculating the National Minimum Wage or National Living Wage. No other company benefit (such as childcare vouchers, meals, or a car) counts towards the National Minimum Wage or National Living Wage.

What doesn't count towards the National Minimum Wage

An employee might be paid at a higher rate than their standard pay rate for some of the work they do – for example for working:

- overtime, weekend or night shifts
- on bank holidays
- longer than a certain number of hours.

If the employee is, the premium element of pay – that is, the amount the higher pay rate exceeds the basic rate – does not count towards their minimum wage pay. The employer also cannot count the following towards the minimum wage pay:

- tips or gratuities
- service charges
- cover charges from customers.

However, an employer can include incentive payments or bonuses as part of the basic pay.

What to do if you think you've been paid less than the correct minimum wage

If you think you've been paid less than the correct minimum wage for your age, talk to your employer directly.

If this doesn't solve the problem, you can ask to see your payment records and make copies of them. You can contact the ACAS helpline for free, confidential advice to help you solve your payment dispute. You can also make a complaint to HMRC about your employer.

If HMRC find that you've been paid incorrectly, your employer must pay you any amounts they owe you and pay a fine to HMRC for paying below the minimum wage.

What is the Living Wage?

The Living Wage is set by the Living Wage Foundation. There is a UK rate and a London rate. The UK Living Wage is £8.75 an hour and the London Living Wage is £10.20 an hour. The Living Wage is based on the cost of living. The Resolution Foundation (a think tank that aims to improve the living standards of low and middle-income families) calculates the rates, and is overseen by the Living Wage Foundation.

Employers don't have to pay the Living Wage, but over 3,600 employers choose to do so.

What's the difference between the National Living Wage and the Living Wage?

The National Living Wage:

- is the highest rate of the National Minimum wage (currently £7.83 an hour)
- is set by government
- must be paid to all workers over 25

The Living Wage:

- is set by the Living Wage Foundation
- applies to all worker over 18
- is voluntary – employers can choose whether to pay it
- has two rates – a UK rate (£8.75 an hour), and a London rate (£10.20 an hour)

*

To treat employees with trust and confidence

In Courtaulds Northern Textiles Ltd v Andrew (1978) the EAT held'---there is an implied term in a contract of employment that employers will not, without reasonable and proper cause, conduct themselves in a manner calculated or likely to destroy or seriously

82

damage the relationship of trust or confidence between the parties' A series of cases have firmly established this principle.

To observe provisions relating to holidays

The written statement provided to employees under the 1996 Act ought to state the holidays to which the employee is entitled and whether the employee is entitled to holiday pay and if so how much. There are relatively few statutory provisions. Section 94 of the Factories Act 1961 provides that women and young persons who work in factories must have a holiday on bank holidays and the Wages Councils and Agricultural Wages Board have the power to fix holiday pay for workers in the industries over which they have jurisdiction.

To observe provisions relating to hours of work

The hours which an employee is required to work are determined by reference to his individual contract of employment and the written statement supplied to the employee ought to state these. There are certain statutory provisions, section 7 of the Sex Discrimination Act 1986 (now replaced by the Equality Act 2010) removed the majority of limitations imposed concerning the hours to be worked by women. Part V1 of the Factories Act 1961 limits the working day to no more than nine hours for young people.

In addition, see below, the Working Time Regulations 1998. These have introduced specific regulations controlling the working week and covers a broad variety of workers not only employees.

To permit employees time off work for public duties

The 1996 Act provides that an employer must permit an employee to have time off work for the purpose of carrying out work as:

a) Justice of the peace (work relating to this)

83

b) a member of a local authority

c) a member of a statutory tribunal

d) a member of a regional health authority or an Area or District educational establishment.

e) a member of a governing body of a local authority maintained educational establishment.

A number of categories of employees are excluded from this right, under the 1996 Act. Under the 1996 Act a pregnant employee has the right not to be unreasonably refused time off work with pay in order that she may keep appointments for receiving anti-natal care. Evidence of pregnancy and appointment must be produced if requested by employer.

To indemnify employees

An employer is under an obligation to indemnify his employees in respect of any expenses incurred in performing their duties under the contract of employment, for example traveling expenses. In certain circumstances however, the employee may be under an obligation to indemnify the employer for any loss sustained: see Lister v Romford Ice and Cold Storage LTD (1957)

To provide references

As we have seen in chapter one, there is no obligation on an employer to supply character references for employees although, in practice, employers normally supply them since failure to provide one speaks for itself. The legal effect of references means that if an employer does provide one, it ought to be correct for several reasons: If a reference is defamatory, the defamed employee may bring an action against the employer, although the defence of qualified privilege is available to the employer, i.e. the employer may show that the statements were made without malice.

84

Negligent misstatement. A person who acts in reliance on a reference, which has been issued negligently, may apparently bring an action to recover any loss sustained as a consequence.

Working Time Rights
Under Europe's Working Time Directive, most people now have seven basic rights to proper time off, rest breaks and paid holiday.

Who has working time rights?
These working time rights apply to all employees and workers from the first day of employment. The rights apply to most agency workers, homeworkers and freelancers. Only those who are self-employed and are genuinely running their own business do not have the right to paid annual leave.

Working time rights do not apply to:

- individuals who are self-employed and who are genuinely running their own business
- individuals who can choose freely their hours and duration of work (such as a managing executive)
- the armed forces, emergency services and police are excluded in some circumstances
- domestic servants in private houses

Working time rules also apply differently to some groups of workers (e.g. those who have to travel a long distance from home to get to work) and in some sectors or workplaces (e.g. security, hospitals, or air, road or sea transport) or when there is an emergency or accident.

Rest breaks

You have the right to a rest break of at least 20 minutes where you work for a continuous period of six hours or more during a working day / shift. If you are under 18 however, you are entitled to a 30-minute break after working four and a half hours.

Additional or longer breaks may be provided for in your contract. A lunch break or coffee break can count as a rest break. The requirements are:

- the break must be in one block
- it cannot be taken off one end of the working day - it must be somewhere in the middle
- you are allowed to spend it away from the workplace

Your employer can say when rest breaks can be taken provided they meet these requirements.

You do not have an automatic right to be paid for rest breaks. Whether you receive pay for rest breaks will depend on your contract.

Daily rest periods

You have the right to a rest period of 11 uninterrupted hours every working day.

If you are under 18, you are entitled to a 12 hour uninterrupted rest period per working day. This rest period must be continuous and uninterrupted.

Weekly rest breaks

You have the right to a rest period of either:
- 24 hours in every 7 day period or
- 48 hours in every fortnight

This rest period must be continuous and uninterrupted. Employers have a duty to make sure that you take your breaks.

48 hour working time limit

You have the right not to work more than 48 hours a week on average. This limit is averaged over a 17-week period. This means that it is legal to work more than 48 hours in some weeks, so long as you work less in others.

You can opt out of this right unless you work at night, but should not be pressured to opt out. The opt-out must be voluntary and must be in writing.

You have a right to opt back in again to working time protection at anytime, but you must give your employer at least 7 days notice. You may be required to give more notice - up to 3 months, if you previously agreed to this with your employer in writing.

Young workers and working time limits

The weekly working time limits for young workers are 8 hours a day and 40 hours per week.

For the majority of young workers these are absolute limits. A young worker's working time is not averaged over a reference period, so in one week they must not work more than 40 hours. The opt-out provisions do not apply to young workers. Young workers will only be able to work more than 8 hours per day, or 40 hours per week if they are needed to:

- keep the continuity of service or production
- respond to a surge in demand for a service or product

And provided that:

- there is no adult available to do the work
- their training needs are not negatively affected

For further detailed information about your working time rights and how these can be enforced please see the TUC guide, 'Enforcing your Basic Workplace Rights'.

What counts as working time?

As well as time spent doing your job, your working time will include time spent on:

- job related training
- job related travelling time, although not time spent travelling
- overtime, whether paid or unpaid
- time spent 'on-call' at the workplace
- working lunches
- time spent working abroad if you work for a UK- based company

What does not count as working time?

Your working time does not include:

- breaks when no work is done, e.g. lunch breaks
- time when you are on-call away from the workplace (although time spent working when away from the workplace, e.g. answering calls at home, will count as working time)
- paid or unpaid holidays

Working in more than one job

If you work for more than one employer, the combined time that you work should not exceed more than 48 hours, unless you have signed the opt out with your employers.

Night work

Regular night workers should not work more than eight hours in each 24-hour period. The Working Time Regulations allow for night work to be averaged over a 17-week period in the same way as weekly hours of work. Please note that there is no opt out from the night work limits.

If your night work involves special hazards or heavy physical or mental strain, you cannot be made to work more than eight hours in any 24 hour period.

Young workers under 18 are not permitted to work between 10pm-6am.

Before night work can commence an employer must have offered you an opportunity to undertake a free health assessment unless you have previously had a health assessment which is still valid.

Your employer must then offer you free health assessments at regular intervals, to ensure it is still safe for you to undertake night work.

Where an employer is advised by a doctor/registered medical practitioner that you cannot undertake night work, the employer should where possible, transfer you to work which they are suited and is work within normal working time (day time).

It is good practice for your employer to provide you with enhanced pay rates for doing night work or unsocial hours. But you will not have a right to receive enhanced pay for doing night work, unless your contract provides for it.

What can I do if I am not allowed to take rest breaks or am asked to work excessive hours?

If your employer does not permit you to take rest breaks or daily or weekly breaks, you can make a complaint to an Employment Tribunal. If your employer pressurises you to work more than 48 hours when you have not signed an opt-out or does not comply with night work rules, you can make a complaint through the Pay and Work Rights helpline.

It is always a good idea to seek advice from your union rep or from the ACAS Helpline before taking steps to enforce your rights.

Holiday pay

If you work regular hours and get the same pay each week, then holiday pay is simply the same as your normal pay. If your normal pay includes regular bonuses, shift premiums or contractual overtime payments, then these should also be included in your holiday pay.

If your weekly pay varies because your hours vary from week to week, then your weekly holiday pay should be the average weekly pay you earned over the last 12 weeks. An interesting case relating to holiday pay is The Sash Windows Workshop Ltd v and Another v King (ECJ) 2015 where a salesperson agreed with his company that he would be self-employed, rather than be engaged on an employment contract. Crucially, this meant that he was not given annual leave. After he retired he claimed that he was owed 13 years backdated holiday pay because he was really a worker. The case went to the ECJ, which concluded that the onus is on the employer to provide paid annual leave to individuals who are really 'workers' regardless of how they are labelled and whether or not the ask for paid leave.

Holiday pay paid throughout the year

When paid holidays were first introduced in 1998, some people found a change to their pay slip. Their take home pay was still the same, but now made up of two elements. First was their basic pay, which had been reduced from what it had been in previous pay packets. The difference was made up with a new element called holiday pay. The employer then said that there was no need for paid holidays as you were getting your holiday pay throughout the year and should save up for it.

Paying holiday pay in this way is now illegal in Scotland but still legal in England and Wales. However, the amount specified must be a genuine addition. See the next chapter for more about holiday pay entitlement.

Special hazards

If your work involves special hazards or heavy physical or mental strain, and you are a night worker, then you cannot work more than eight hours in any 24. This is not an average but an absolute limit. In other words as soon as you have worked eight hours then you must stop.

****

Chapter 6

Pay and Conditions

Payment for work is one of the most contentious areas of employment and it is necessary for any employee to have at least a basic knowledge of their overall entitlement.

Remuneration

A number of legislative provisions exist, affecting remuneration to employees and the way it is paid: the 2010 Equality Act; The Wages Act 1986, consolidated by the 1996 Employment Rights Act and the National Minimum Wage Act 1998. In addition, the 2002 Employment Act has introduced changes to rights of parents and their remuneration. See below.

Payslips

Two new statutory instruments will take effect from April 2019. In consequence of the Employment Rights Act 1996 (Itemised pay Stament) (Amendment) Order 2018 all payslips must state the number of hours being paid where wages vary according to time worked and also all workers will have the right to a written pay statement and the ability to enforce that right before a tribunal should the employer not comply.

The Equality Act 2010

An Act which affects equal pay is the Equality Act 2010. Under this Act it is unlawful for an employer to discriminate against a person because of their sex. This is wide ranging and covers everything from recruitment, employment terms and conditions, pay and benefits, training, promotion, redundancy and dismissal. For the purposes of this chapter, where men and women, working for the same employer, are doing one of the following they are entitled to the same terms in their employment contract:

- The same or similar work
- Work rated as equivalent in a job evaluation study by the employer
- Work of equal value. Pay secrecy clauses in a contract are unenforceable, if an employee or other is trying to find out if any difference in pay is connected with a protected characteristic, for example, sex.

Gender pay gap reporting

To address the gender pay gap, the Government has introduced, from April 2017, a completely new requirement for all large organisations to publish their gender pay gap. Employers will need to publish key wage information, and these details will need to include the difference in hourly earnings as well as the gap in bonus pay.

Acts generally

The scope of the various Acts is wide. By S8 of the 1996 Act every employee who works eight hours or more a week has the right to an itemised pay statement. It must state the gross and net amount of pay and the amounts deducted and the purpose of the deduction.

The 2010 Equality Act provides that all employees doing the same job be paid equal wages or salary. The 1986 Wages Act, now consolidated by the 1996 Act defined wages in very broad terms. Wages means 'any sum payable to a worker by his employer in connection with his employment and includes any fee, bonus commission, holiday pay or other emolument referable to his employment, whether payable under his contract or otherwise...' However, a number of payments are specifically excluded and these include expenses and redundancy payments.

One of the effects of the 1986 Wages Act was to abolish the requirement that workers be paid in 'coin of the realm'. We now have the concept of cash-less pay. The 1996 Act only allows deductions from wages if made by virtue of a statutory provision or by a provision of the workers contract, or if the work has previously indicated his agreement in writing to it. There are much stricter controls on retail workers who are defined as being workers who carry out retail transactions directly with members of the public or with fellow workers. Under the Act any deductions in respect of cash shortages or stock deficiencies must not exceed one tenth of the gross amount of wages payable on that day. Also, any sum demanded of such a worker in respect of these losses shall not exceed the 10% figure.

Guarantee payments

Unless a contract of employment expressly or implicitly allows for it, an employee who is laid off is entitled to be paid during the period of such lay off.

To be eligible to receive such a payment, an employee must:

a) have been continuously employed for at least one month when the lay off occurs;
b) have been laid off for the whole of his working hours on a day he is normally required to work;
c) not have unreasonably refused an offer of alternative employment, which was suitable in all the circumstances;
d) have complied with any reasonable requirements imposed by the

employer with a view to ensuring that his services are available;

e) not have been laid off because of a strike, lock out or other industrial action involving any employee of the employer or of any associated employer; and

f) have been available for employment on that day.

An employee who is entitled to a guarantee payment is entitled to be paid at the guaranteed hourly rate, subject to a maximum limit for one day. There is a maximum entitlement of five guarantee payments in any period of three months.

Suspension from work on medical grounds

The legislation governing suspension from work on medical grounds was SS 19-22 of the 1978 Act as amended by the Employment Act 1982 consolidated by the Employment Rights Act 1996 (s 64).

The above Act provides that an employee who is suspended from work is entitled to be paid by his employer if that suspension is in consequence of a requirement imposed under certain statutory provisions or a recommendation made in a Code of Practice issued or approved under s 16 of the Health and Safety at Work Act 1974. There are certain eligibility criteria concerning length of employment etc. An employee is entitled to be paid for up to twenty-six weeks of such suspension after one month's employment. An important case in relation to sick leave is that of O'Brien v Bolton St Catherine's Academy (Court of Appeal) 2017 in which the court of appeal provided guidance on when employers can dismiss and employee on long term sick leave.

Provisions relating to sick pay

An employer may have an obligation by virtue of a term in the contract of employment to pay sick pay to employees. Such an obligation may arise as a result of an express term or an obligation may arise under an implied term. The principles governing the implication of terms relating to sick pay were discussed by the court of appeal in Mears v Safecar Security Ltd (1982) where it was held that there is no general presumption of an implied right to sick pay.

Since April 1983 all employers have had a statutory obligation under the Social Security and Housing Benefits Act 1982 to pay Statutory Sick Pay to their employees. The employer pays the employee his statutory sick pay and, until recently then recouped those payments through his National Insurance Contributions.

By the Statutory Sick Pay Act 1994 only those employers who pay less than £2000 in National Insurance contributions can now recoup such payments.

In outline the scheme provides that a qualifying employee is entitled to SSP for the first 28 weeks of sickness (there is no entitlement for the first three days, called 'waiting days') and after that period he will receive state sickness benefit. Certain employees are excluded from the scheme, including pensioners, persons employed for less than three months, persons who do not pay NI contributions and persons who are not employed due to a trade union dispute at their workplace.

More about sick pay

A person may be able to get sick pay if they have been sick for at least four or more days in a row (including weekends, bank holidays and days that you do not normally work). In addition, average weekly earnings were equal to more than the Lower Earnings Limit (LEL). The LEL is the amount a person needs to earn before paying National Insurance Contributions. From 6th April 2018 this was £117 per week.

From April 2018, you must have average earnings of £117 per week before tax and National Insurance contributions are deducted.

Average weekly earnings are calculated over the eight weeks before your sickness began. Only earnings paid in this eight week period can be used for the average weekly earnings.

Sick pay and holidays

One of the most confusing areas of employment law in recent years has concerned the impact of sickness absence on employees' entitlement to statutory holiday and holiday pay.

These issues have been examined at judicial levels from Employment Tribunals to the European Court of Justice. Some key points that have emerged from these cases are set out below:

- Employees on sickness absence during a holiday year do not lose their entitlement to accrue annual leave.
- While on sickness absence, an employee can nominate a period of the sick leave as holiday and should be paid at the full contractual rate.
- An employee on long term sickness absence who does not wish to nominate a period of sick leave as annual leave is entitled to carry the accrued annual leave forward into the next holiday year. However, leave carried forward in these circumstances should be taken within 18 months of the end of the leave year in which it was accrued.
- If prearranged holiday coincides with sick leave the employee should be allowed to take the holiday at another time.
- On termination of employment, an employee is entitled to payment in lieu of accrued holiday that has been carried over, where the carried over leave relates to a holiday year in which they were absent for the entire year due to sickness.

Agency workers

If agency workers meet the qualifying conditions for payment then it will be payable. It remains payable whilst you are working for your agency. The employer cannot end the contract of service to avoid paying SSP. Whoever is responsible for the deduction of National Insurance contributions from your earnings is also responsible for payment of SSP.

Telling the employer that you are sick and providing evidence

Before the employer can decide on entitlement to SSP, they must be told that you are sick and you must provide evidence. The employer may have their own rules about telling them when you are sick. If they don't, the following will apply:

- The employer should be informed within seven days of the first day that you are sick
- The employer cannot insist that you tell them in person, earlier than the first qualifying day or by a set time, on a special form, on a doctor's statement of fitness for work (fit note) which was previously called a medical certificate or sick note
- More than once a week during your sickness.

The 'fit note' replaced the doctor's sick note on 6th April 2010.

Your employer does not have to pay SSP for any delay in telling them that you are sick. They will pay from the date that they were told as long as you are still sick and the rules for payment are satisfied.

Evidence that you are sick

It is up to your employer to decide whether you are incapable of work for payment of SSP. Your employer cannot ask you to provide medical evidence that you are sick for the first seven days of illness. During this period they may ask you to fill in a self-certificate of their own design or form SC2. If you are sick for more than seven days, your employer can ask you to give them some medical evidence from your doctor. This is used to support payment of SSP.

A 'fit note' from your doctor that says you are not fit for work is strong evidence of sickness. If your employer has strong reasons to believe that you are not sick, they can refuse to pay SSP. They can refuse even if they have strong evidence from your doctor. To help them decide whether or not to pay sick pay, with your consent the employer can get a medical; report from:

- Your doctor
- Their own medical advisors
- A Medical Service Provider through Her Majesty's Revenue and Customs (HMRC).

Holiday pay
Calculating holiday pay
In addition to legislation, a number of recent court judgments should be taken into account when calculating holiday pay for the 4 weeks of annual leave required by the EU Working Time Directive.

Key points
- Workers should usually receive the same pay while they are on annual leave as they normally receive while they are at work. All types of overtime, including voluntary, must be included when calculating a worker's statutory holiday pay entitlement, apart from overtime that is only worked on a genuinely occasional and infrequent basis. Commission should be factored into statutory holiday pay calculations.

99

- Work-related travel may need to be factored into statutory holiday pay calculations.
- A worker's entitlement to holiday pay will continue to accrue during sick leave and maternity or parental leave.
- There are different rules for calculating holiday pay depending on the working patterns involved.
- Workers must take their statutory paid annual leave allowance and can only be 'paid in lieu' for this when their employment ends.

General principle of holiday pay

In general, workers should receive the same pay while they are on annual leave as they normally receive while they are at work. They should not be deterred from taking leave because they are paid less while they are on leave. This principle only applies to the 4 weeks of annual leave required by the EU Working Time Directive. All workers also receive a further 1.6 weeks of annual leave required by UK law, and some receive additional amounts as a part of their contracts too. Many employers choose to apply the judgments to this extra annual leave. Doing this is not a legal requirement but can help to keep their processes simple and understandable.

Limit on a claim for an underpayment

The Deduction from Wages (Limitation) Regulations 2014 means that a claim for backdated deductions from wages for holiday pay made on or after 1st July 2015 are subject to a two year cap. This means that the period that the claim can cover will be limited to a maximum of 2 years.

Commission

Commission is usually an amount of money a worker receives as a result of making sales and can make up some or all of their earnings. Results based commission must be factored into holiday payments for the 4 weeks of statutory annual leave required under European law. There is no requirement to do this for the additional 1.6 weeks of statutory annual leave provided under UK law, or for any additional contractual annual leave allowance. This was confirmed on 22 May 2014 when the European Court of Justice heard the case of Lock v British Gas Trading Ltd.

Work-related travel

Work-related travel can have a number of different meanings but for most employment matters, this will usually mean any travel that is made for work purposes that is not a part of a workers commute to their usual place of work. On 4 November 2014 the Employment Appeal Tribunal issued a judgment in a case joined to Bear Scotland v Fulton which covers how holiday pay should be calculated in relation to work-related travel.

Where payments are made for time spent travelling to and from work as part of a worker's normal pay, these may need to be considered when calculating holiday pay.

Holiday pay and sickness

When a worker takes paid or unpaid sick leave, their annual leave will continue to accrue. If a worker is unable to take their annual leave in their current leave year because of sickness, they should be allowed to carry that annual leave over until they are able to take it, or they may choose to specify a period where they are sick but still wish to be paid annual leave at their usual annual leave rate.

Calculating holiday pay for different working patterns

No matter the working pattern, a worker should still receive holiday pay based on a 'week's normal remuneration'. This usually means their weekly wage but may include allowances or similar payments.

101

Some of these payments might include the situations described earlier on this page, such as commission.

For workers with fixed working hours - If a worker's working hours do not vary, holiday pay would be a week's normal remuneration. For workers with no normal working hours - If a worker has no normal working hours then their holiday pay would still be a week's normal remuneration but the week's pay is usually calculated by working out the average pay received over the previous 12 weeks in which they were paid.

For shift workers - If a worker works shifts then a week's holiday pay is usually calculated by working out the average number of hours worked in the previous 12 weeks at their average hourly rate.

Payment in lieu of holidays

While workers are in employment, 5.6 weeks of their annual leave (this is the amount all UK workers are statutorily entitled to) must be taken and cannot be 'paid off'. Anything above the statutory allowance may be paid in lieu but this would depend on the terms of the contract. When a worker's employment is terminated, all outstanding holiday pay that has been accrued but not taken (including the statutory allowance) must be paid.

Maternity and parental pay and leave

Apart from important protection from unfair dismissal because of pregnancy, the Employment Rights Act 1996 provided four further protections in relation to pregnancy - the right to maternity leave, the right to return to work after maternity leave, the right to time off for ante-natal care and the right to maternity pay. The section of the above Act dealing with maternity leave was replaced in its entirety by the Employment Relations Act 1999 Part 1, Schedule 4 which in turn has been amended by the 2002 Employment Act, the provisions of which came into force on April 6th 2003. An

102

amendment was also made by the Maternity and Parental Leave Regulations 2008. and also the parental Leave (EU Directive) Regulations 2013.

In addition to the above, pregnancy and maternity is now one of the protected characteristics in the Equality Act 2010 and there is now implied into every woman's term of employment a maternity equality clause (s 73 Equality Act 2010). The Act protects women from direct discrimination (s 13(1)) and indirect discrimination (s 19(1)) in relation to pregnancy and maternity.

Right to maternity leave

Part V111 of the 1996 Employment Rights Act contains provisions for maternity rights that are further detailed in the Maternity and Parental Leave Regulations 1999. The Directive gives all pregnant employees a general right to maternity leave.

Under the 1999 Employment Rights Act, which came into force on the 15th December 1999, the periods of leave were renamed. Maternity leave became ordinary maternity leave (OML) and additional absence became additional maternity leave (AML).

The regulations now clarify that the term remuneration is now limited to 'sums payable by way of wages or salary'. This means, for example, that women will automatically be entitled to retain a company car and a mobile phone and to receive a performance bonus which is not salary.

All pregnant employees are entitled to 52 weeks maternity leave. This consists of 26 weeks Ordinary Maternity Leave and 26 weeks Additional Maternity Leave. This is available to all employees from the first day of employment. The employee can choose when they start their leave but the earliest it can start is 11 weeks before the baby is due. The only women not entitled to maternity leave are:

*   Share fisherwomen

103

- Women who normally work abroad (unless they have a work connection with the UK
- Policewomen and women serving in the armed forces

Compulsory maternity leave

An employer may not permit an employee to work during her compulsory maternity period. Compulsory maternity leave is a period of two weeks commencing on the day on which childbirth occurs. An employer who allows a pregnant person to work can be fined.

Giving notice to the employer

In order to qualify for maternity leave the employer must be informed by the end of the 15th week before the baby is due:

- that the employee is pregnant
- the week in which the baby is expected; and
- the date when the employee intends to start ordinary maternity leave.

There is no obligation to put this in writing unless asked to. However, it is a good idea to do so. Once the employer has been informed that maternity leave will be taken they have 28 days to inform you when maternity leave starts. If the employee has already a contractual right to maternity pay/leave, she may exercise her right to the more favourable terms. If there is a redundancy situation during the leave period and it is not practicable because of the redundancy for the employer to continue to employ her under her existing contract, she is entitled to be offered a suitable vacancy before her employment ends. If a woman intends to return to work before the end of maternity leave, 56 days notice must be given. Since women who qualify now have the right to take Additional
104

Maternity Leave, and there is no obligation to notify the employer during the initial notification, then until notification of a return to work is given, the women will retain the right to return but not pay.

Work during the maternity leave period
Regulation 12A provides that an employee may carry out up to ten days work for her employer during her statutory maternity period (excluding the compulsory maternity period) without bringing her maternity period to an end.

Time off for Ante-natal care
To qualify for this right the employee must have made an appointment for ante-natal care on the advice of a doctor, midwife or health visitor. The employer may not refuse time off for the first visit, but for further appointments, the employer may ask for a certificate or appointment card or other evidence.

Statutory Maternity Pay
The Social Security Act of 1996 and the Statutory Maternity Pay regulations of the same year entitle certain employees to statutory maternity pay. This has been amended by the 2002 Employment Act. SMP is paid for a maximum of 39 weeks. For the first six weeks of maternity leave SMP is paid at 90% of the average gross weekly earnings (before tax and NI) for the remaining 33 weeks it is paid at 90% of gross weekly earnings or £145.18 (2018-19) a week, whichever is the lower.

To claim SMP, a person must tell their employer, 28 days before maternity leave, that they are pregnant and will be off work because of birth. A medical certificate has to be provided.

When is SMP paid?
How long SMP is paid for depends on when the baby is due. It is

paid up to 39 weeks. The earliest a person can start maternity leave and start to get SMP is 11 weeks before the baby is due. The latest date to start maternity leave and receiving SMP is the week after the week when the baby is born. If a person is sick with a pregnancy related illness before the baby is due, SMP will start the week following the week that sickness began. If a person is sick with a non-pregnancy related illness they can claim Statutory Sick pay until the week that the baby is due.

Maternity Allowance

If an employee is not entitled to get SMP they may be entitled to maternity allowance instead. This is administered through jobcentre plus and a person might get maternity benefit if:

- they are employed, but not eligible for SMP
- they are registered self-employed and paying class C National Insurance Contributions (NIC's) or hold a Small Earnings Exemption Certificate
- they have been very recently employed or self-employed.

Further, they may be eligible if:
- they have been employed or self employed for at least 26 weeks in the 'test period' (66 weeks up to and including the week before the week the baby is due) part weeks count as full weeks; and
- they earned £30 a week averaged over any 13 week period in the test period.

Returning to work after maternity leave

There is an automatic right to return to work after maternity leave and it is assumed the person will do so unless they state otherwise. If a person decides to return earlier than the date notified by the employer, then at least 56 days notice must be given of returning.

Parental leave

The Maternity and Parental Leave Regulations 1999 provide that every person who cares for a young child, or has recently adopted a child, can take time off from work at his or her own convenience to care for that child. Minimum provisions are set for leave, preconditions are set for leave and the notice that an employee has to give an employer before leave can be taken is set out. Employers and employees can agree to vary these provisions by using a workforce agreement as long as it is equal to or more favorable than the statutory provisions.

Any employee who has one year's continuous employment at the date the leave is due to start, and who has, or expects to have, responsibility for a child at that time can apply to take parental leave. A person will have responsibility for a child under the regulations if he/she has parental responsibility under the Children Act 1989 or is registered as the father under the provision of the Births and Deaths Register Act.

The leave entitlement is up to 4 weeks unpaid parental leave per year while the child is under the age of 5, subject to an overall maximum of 18 weeks leave in respect of each child. If there are twins, each parent can take 26 weeks parental leave. The leave for the parent of a disabled child is 18 weeks per child. the leave for parents of an adopted child is 18 weeks up to their 18th birthday or 5th anniversary of their adoption, whichever comes first.

Employers can request records of leave already taken with previous employers; the entitlement is per child and not per employer. The employee can take leave in blocks of 1 week (or blocks of one day where the child is disabled) to a maximum of 4 weeks in respect of an individual child in an individual year. (Part time employees get a pro-rata entitlement.)

107

Paternity leave

In addition, the 2002 Employment Act widened the scope and range of paternity leave. The Act introduced the right to two weeks paid leave in addition to the 13 weeks unpaid leave. This became effective from April 2003. Leave must be taken within 8 weeks of the birth of the child or placement of the child through adoption.

For employees to claim paternity leave they must:

- Be employed and have worked for their employer for at least 26 weeks before the end of the 15th week before the expected week of childbirth; and
- Be the biological father of the child, or be married to or be the partner of the baby's mother (this includes same sex partners, whether or not they are registered civil partners); and
- Have some responsibility for the child's upbringing; and
- Have given the employer the correct notice to take paternity leave.
- Paternity leave can be taken as a single block of either one or two weeks.

All terms and conditions of employment remain intact during the period of paternity leave except the right to remuneration. Employees are entitled to return to the jobs they had before they took paternity leave.

The Additional Paternity Leave Regulations 2010

The Additional Paternity Leave Regulations 2010 recognised that mothers can often be the main earner for the family and aims to promote shared parenting. The regulations enabled eligible employees to have the right to take additional paternity leave and

108

pay. However the right only affected parents of children that were due to be born on or after the 3rd April 2011 or where one or both of the parents had received adoptive notification on or after the 3rd April 2011 that they have been matched with a child for adoption.

Additional Paternity Leave (APL) allowed a father to take up to 26 weeks leave to care for a child and also allowed mothers to 'transfer' up to 6 months of maternity leave to their partner. APL started 20 weeks after the birth of the child and ended no later then the child's first birthday.

However, Additional Paternity Leave is to be replaced by Shared parental leave for babies born on or after April 5th 2015. Therefore, for the purposes of this book we will refer to the new regulations outlined below.

Shared parental leave

Shared parental leave is available for babies with an expected week of childbirth (EWC) starting on or after 5 April 2015. The new right is governed by the Shared Parental Leave Regulations 2014, in force from 1 December 2014. The following deals with the main features of the draft regulations; the detail could, of course, change when the final regulations are published.

A woman, who is eligible for shared parental leavel has the right to bring her maternity leave and pay period to an end early and convert the outstanding period of maternity leave and pay into a period of shared parental leave and pay that can be taken by either parent. Shared parental leave can be taken in a more flexible way than maternity leave. It does not have to be a single continuous period; leave periods can be as little as a week and both parents can be absent from work at the same time.

Shared parental leave must be taken before the child's first birthday and is in addition to the right to unpaid parental leave under the Maternity and Parental Leave Regulations 1999. The existing right to additional paternity leave is replaced by the new right to shared parental leave, although remains in place for babies with an EWC starting before 5 April 2015.

A parent taking adoption leave also has the right to convert a period of adoption leave into a period of shared parental leave which either parent can take in a flexible way if they have a matching date on or after 5 April 2015. Below are the main points of the new regulationsThe right to shared parental leave applies to babies with an expected week of childbirth starting on or after 5 April 2015.The default position remains that a woman is entitled to 52 weeks' maternity leave and 39 weeks' maternity pay. However, a woman on maternity leave can commit to bringing her maternity leave and pay period to an end early. The balance of the maternity leave and pay period becomes available for either parent to take as shared parental leave and pay. hared parental leave can be taken in periods of a week or multiples of a week at a time.A parent can take a period of shared parental leave at the same time that the other parent is on maternity leave or shared parental leave.A parent will only qualify to take shared parental leave if the other parent meets basic work and earnings criteria and the parent taking the leave meets the individual eligibility criteria (such as having 26 weeks' continuous service at the 15th week before the EWC and remaining in the same employment).

- An employer must have at least eight weeks' notice of any period of shared parental leave.
- Each parent can make up to three requests for periods of shared parental leave. Whether the employer can refuse a request depends on whether the employee has asked for a continuous or discontinuous period of leave.
- Sp leave has to be taken before the child's first birthday

Rights during a period of shared parental leave mirror those of a woman on maternity leave: all terms and conditions of employment continue except those relating to remuneration.

If employees suffer any detrimental treatment or are dismissed as a result of taking or asking to take shared parental leave they can bring a complaint to the employment tribunal.

Shared Parental Pay

From April 2018, Statutory Shared Parental Pay is paid at £145.18 or 90% of an employee's average weekly earnings (whichever is lower).

If the mother or adopter curtails their entitlement to maternity/adoption pay or maternity allowance before they have used their full entitlement then Statutory Shared Parental Pay can be claimed for any remaining weeks.

To qualify for Statutory Shared Parental Pay a parent must pass the continuity of employment test and have earned an average salary of the lower earnings limit of £116 for the 8 weeks' prior to the 15th week before the expected due date or matching date. The other parent in the family must meet the employment and earnings test.

A couple of interesting cases to note, in relation to shared parental leave, are Ali v Capita Customer management Ltd (Employment Tribunal) 2018. Capita Customer Management's relevant maternity policy granted women the right to 14 weeks' enhanced pay whilst on maternity leave, However, its Shared Parental Leave policy allowed partners statutory shared parental pay only.

When his wife was diagnosed with postnatal depression and was advised to return to work to aid her recovery, Mr Ali took Shared Parental Leave to care for their new-born baby. When he was paid statutory shared parental leave pay only during his period of leave, Mr Ali complained to an employment tribunal that his employer had treated him less favourably than its female employees. The tribunal agreed.

In the other case Hextall v Leicestershire Police 2018 the police force paid enhanced maternity pay to women on maternity leave for up to 18 weeks. Shared parental pay was paid at the statutory rate only. A male police officer who had taken Shared Parental Leave claimed that this was sex discrimination. His claim failed, because the tribunal found that a father on shared parental leave could not compare himself with a woman on maternity leave. The proper comparator was someone in the same circumstances as the man - such as the same sex partner of a child's mother who was taking Shared Parental Leave. As that person (a woman) would not receive enhanced pay either, the sex discrimination claim had to fail.

Adoption leave and pay
Qualifying employees who have been matched with a child may take up to 52 weeks adoption leave, and may be entitled to 39 weeks of statutory adoption pay. If a couple jointly adopt a child, one may take adoption leave and the other parent may be able to take paternity leave or shared parental leave.

Key points
- The main adopter will be able to take paid time off for up to five adoption appointments.
- The secondary adopter will be entitled to take unpaid time off for up to two appointments. Adoption leave is a "day one" right there is no qualifying period.
- Statutory Adoption Pay - the first six weeks will be paid at 90% of the employee's normal earnings.
- Some surrogate parents will become eligible for adoption leave.

Adoption leave may be taken:

- When a child starts living with the employee or up to 14 days before the placement date (UK adoptions).
- When an employee has been matched with a child by a UK adoption agency.
- When the child arrives in the UK or within 28 days (overseas adoption).

The partner of an individual who adopts, or the secondary adopter if a couple are adopting jointly may be entitled to paternity leave and pay or shared parental leave. Employees must give their employer documentary proof to show that they have the right to paid Statutory Adoption Leave. This is usually a matching certificate from the adoption agency. The adoption agency must be recognised in the UK.

Statutory adoption leave can start either:

- from the date the child starts living with the employee
- up to 14 days before the date the child is expected to start living with the employee.
- Employees should tell the employer within seven days of being told that they have been matched with a child, if this is not possible they must tell the employer as soon as possible.

Employees who request or take adoption leave are protected against suffering a detriment or unfair dismissal. They have a right to return to the same job after 26 weeks adoption leave and after 52 weeks a suitable alternative job must be found.

Statutory Adoption Pay

. For the first six weeks the employee will be entitled to 90% of their normal earnings. The following 33 weeks will be paid at the

113

statutory adoption pay rate. Some employers may offer to pay more than this - if they do it may form part of the terms and conditions of the employment contract. From April 2018, the rate is £145.18.

Keep in touch day
Both parties should agree when and how the employer will keep in contact, this may be via email, telephone contact etc. Employees should also agree with their employer if they will work the "keeping in touch" days, these can be used for training days, team events etc. Up to ten keeping in touch days can be worked, and there is no provision for these days to be paid, this should be agreed between employee and employer. Statutory Adoption Pay may be paid or this may be off set against any contractual pay agreed.

Bereavement leave
In October 2017, the Government published a bill that will offer two weeks' paid leave for bereaved parents. The Parental Bereavement (Pay and Leave) Bill, will give a day-one right to parental bereavement leave for any employed parent who loses a child under the age of 18. Employees with a minimum of 26 weeks' continuous service will be eligible for statutory parental bereavement pay, for which employers will be able to reclaim some or all of the cost. The bill will receive a second reading in Parliament on 20 October, with the aim of it becoming law in 2020.

The proposals first emerged in the Conservative party manifesto earlier this year. There is currently no legal requirement for employers to provide paid time off for grieving parents, although many do. Under the Employment Rights Act, employees have a day-one right to take a "reasonable" amount of unpaid time off work to deal with an emergency involving a dependant, which could include making arrangements following the death of a dependant.

*

Statutory right to request a contractual variation-flexible working

The 2002 Employment Act introduced a right to request a contractual variation, where the reason for the request relates to a young child. The 2006 Work and Families Act extended the right, from April 2007 to an employee who cares for, or who expects to care for, an adult. A carer is defined as an employee who is, or expects to be, caring for an adult who is married to, or is the partner or civil partner of the employee or who is a near relative of the employee or falls into neither of these categories but lives at the same address as the employer.

Applications can only be made by parents or potential carers who have worked continuously for an employer for 26 weeks before applying From 30 June 2014 every employee has the statutory right to request flexible working after 26 weeks employment service. (Before 30 June 2014, the right only applies to parents of children under the age of 17 (or 18 if the child is disabled) and certain carers.) or by parents of disabled children under the age of 18. An employee can request changes to his or her terms and conditions and, in particular, the following:

- Hours of work
- The times when the employee is required to work.
- Where the employee is required to work
- Such other aspects of his or her terms and conditions of employment as the Secretary of State may specify

Procedure for flexible working request

A request for flexible working must:

- State that it is a request for flexible working'
- Specify the changes applied for and the date on which they are to become effective and:

115

- Explain what effect the changes have on the workplace and how they can propose they can be dealt with
- Only one request can be made per year.

Employer's response

The employer must consider the application and can only refuse the application on certain given grounds. These are as follows:

- The burden of additional costs
- The detrimental effect on ability to meet customer demand
- The inability to reorganize work amongst existing staff
- The detrimental impact on quality
- The detrimental impact on performance
- The insufficiency of work during the period the employee proposes to work: and
- Any planned structural changes

Regulations will provide a timetable detailing how the employer must respond to a request for flexible working.

It is likely that an employer will be required to arrange a meeting to consider the request within 28 days of receipt. The employer must give a decision within 14 days of the meeting. If the employee's request is refused, the employer must give grounds for the decision.

An employee will be entitled to appeal but must set out their grounds for appeal. The employer must hear the appeal within 14 days and a decision must be given to the employee within 14 days of the appeal hearing.

Remedies

Where a request has been refused an employee can bring a claim at the Employment Tribunal but only where the employer:

- Has failed to comply with the statutory procedure in considering the application.
- Has refused the request on a ground that is different to the specified grounds above: or
- Has made the decision based on incorrect facts
- Therefore, there is no jurisdiction for the Employment Tribunal to hear a claim if the employee is merely unhappy about the decision.

If the Tribunal finds against the employer it can:

- Order reconsideration of the issue and/or
- Make an award for compensation

In addition, there will also be the right for employees not to be subjected to a detriment, including dismissal by the employer if they have made an application for flexible working, they have appealed against a refusal to allow flexible working, they have brought proceedings in the Employment Tribunal in respect of a refusal to allow flexible working, or the employee has alleged circumstances which could constitute a ground for bringing such proceedings.

Part Time Workers
There have been significant advances relating to the position of part time workers in relation to remuneration and terms and conditions of employment. The Part-Time Workers (Prevention of Less Favourable Treatment) Regulations 2000 introduced new rights for part time workers. They implement EU Directive 97/81/EC. The Part-Time Workers Regulations ensure that Britain's Part Timers are not treated less favourably than comparable full-timers in their terms and conditions, unless it is objectively justified. This means

117

part-timers are entitled to a range of benefits, including:

- The same hourly rates of pay
- The same access to company pension schemes
- The same entitlements to annual leave and maternity/parental leave on a pro-rata basis
- The same entitlement to contractual sick pay
- No less favourable treatment in access to training

Two amendments in 2002 introduced Comparators and occupational pension schemes (regulation 2).

Under the original regulations, part-timers had to compare themselves to full-timers employed under the same type of contract. This meant that, for example a part-timer on a fixed-term contract should compare themselves to a full-timer on a fixed-term contract. This is no longer the case

The other amendment is that of access to occupational pension schemes. Under Regulation 8 (8) of the Part-Time Workers Regulations, where an Employment Tribunal has upheld a complaint from a part-timer for equal access to an occupational pension scheme, the remedies which the tribunal orders may go back no further than two years. In 2001, the House of Lords (now Supreme Court) held that this was unlawful in that it contravened European law on the equal treatment of men and women, and could no longer be maintained. As a consequence the law has now been amended to remove the two-year time limit.

Pensions

Pension schemes have become increasingly complex over the years and they have also become notably less generous. Pensions organised by the employer are called occupational pensions. There are, however, other types of pensions which are not, strictly speaking, occupational pensions. These are generally pensions to

118

which an employer provides a gateway. The state also provides a range of different pensions. In addition, an employee can also save for retirement through personal or stakeholder pensions. Although there is currently no legal obligation on an employer to set up a pension scheme or to contribute in any way to their employee's pensions, this has changed from 2012. The one main requirement is that all employers with one or more employees who do not provide alternative pension arrangements must automatically enrol certain workers into a pension scheme. The employer must make contributions on their workers behalf, register with the Pensions Regulator and provide workers with basic information and how it will affect them. The new employer duties commenced in 2012 and was introduced in stages over six years. Each employer will be allocated a date from when the duties will first apply to them, known as their staging date. For more details of how the changes affect both employer and employee the pensions regulator website www.thepensionsregulator.gov.uk provides more information.

Rights to information
Members of pension schemes have comprehensive rights to information about their scheme:

- Basic information. This encompasses the broad details of the scheme and should be available on request.
- Annual statements. Members of personal, stakeholder and money purchase occupational schemes should receive annual statements automatically. Members of final salary schemes can request a statement and it should be provided within two months.
- Contributions. If your employer fails for any reason to pay over contributions then the trustees must tell you.

119

- Early leavers. If you leave a pension scheme before you retire, for example when you change a job, you should be given a statement about your options within two months of leaving.
- Payment of benefits. You should automatically be provided with details of your pension before your retirement date.
- Changes to the scheme. You should automatically be told of any changes to the rules of the scheme.
- You can ask to see any paperwork related to the scheme such as the annual report, trust deed and rules schedule of contributions and the transfer value.

Insolvency of employer

For the legislation governing the insolvency of an employer, the Employment Rights Act 1996 applies. See also s 175 and schedule 6 of the Insolvency Act 1986. If an employer becomes insolvent an employee acquires certain rights. He becomes a preferential creditor in respect of up to four months-unpaid wages or a maximum set by the Secretary of State. Certain other payments are also deemed to be preferential debts including guarantee payments, payment for time off for trade union activities and payment for ante -natal care. The employee is entitled to claim payments of certain amounts due to him from his employer from the Secretary of State who will pay them out of the redundancy fund. The classes of debt for which payment may be made include arrears of wages (up to a maximum of 8 weeks) holiday pay (6 weeks) and wages during the statutory minimum notice period.

****

Chapter 7

Terminating Employment

There are a number of ways in which a contract of employment may come to an end-termination by way of contract, termination in breach of contract and termination by methods external to the contract.

At common law, a contract of employment can be validly terminated by an employer giving notice to an employee in accordance with the terms of the contract or, in the absence of such a term, by giving reasonable notice. If sufficient notice was given, the employee had no further rights and this meant that dismissal could be entirely arbitrary. However, in recent times provisions have been introduced whereby an employee may be entitled to compensation for loss of job despite the fact that he was given notice.

It should be noted that once notice has been given, it can only effectively be withdrawn with the consent of the other party.

Dismissal with notice

The length of notice, which must be given by an employer to an employee, is determined by reference to the following criteria to be applied in the following order:

a) Express terms of the contract. If the contract of employment expressly provides for a period of notice, this must be observed unless that period is less than the statutory minimum to which that particular employee is entitled under d) below.

b) In the absence of an express term it may be impossible to imply a term into the contract, for example, by custom. Again, such a period may not be less than the statutory custom.

c) If there is no express or implied term of the contract, the courts may rely on a reasonable period. What is "reasonable" depends upon such factors as the status of the employee, salary, length of employment with that employer, age etc. The "reasonable" period cannot be less than the statutory minimum. In the absence of any of the above criteria, or where they produce a period less than the following, the statutory minimum in s 86 of the 1996 Act (ERA) must be applied in respect of those employees covered by that section. Section 86 provides that for an employee continuously employed for between one month and two years, the notice period is one week; for an employee employed for more than two years, he is entitled to one week for each year of continuous employment subject to a maximum of twelve weeks notice after twelve years of employment. These rights do not apply to a contract for the performance of a specific task, which is not expected to last for more than three months.

Constructive dismissal

Constructive dismissal is when you're forced to leave your job against your will because of your employer's conduct.

The reasons you leave your job must be serious, for example, they:

- don't pay you or suddenly demote you for no reason
- force you to accept unreasonable changes to how you work – e.g. tell you to work night shifts when your contract is only for day work
- let other employees harass or bully you

Your employer's breach of contract may be one serious incident or a series of incidents that are serious when taken together. You should try and sort any issues out by speaking to your employer to solve the dispute.

If you do have a case for constructive dismissal, you should leave your job immediately - your employer may argue that, by staying, you accepted the conduct or treatment.

Summary dismissal

Summary dismissal is where an employer dismisses an employee without giving the employee the amount of notice to which that individual is entitled. If there is no justification, such dismissal is wrongful and an action can be brought.

The remedy for wrongful dismissal is damages representing the loss of wages during the period of notice that ought to have been given. In addition, wrongful dismissal may also be unfair dismissal within the meaning of the 1996 Act.

Circumstances which justify summary dismissal

The question of what justifies summary dismissal is not one that can be answered with a simple rule since each case must be decided according to the particular circumstances. However, a general principle has emerged that summary dismissal is justified if the conduct of the employee is such that it prevents further satisfactory continuance of the relationship. This was the finding in Sinclair v Neighbour (1967).

The status of the employee in question is a relevant consideration as is the fact that the employee has a history of misconduct as opposed to an isolated incident.

Dismissals Procedure

If the contract states that dismissal is to be according to an established pattern (e.g. that there will be two warnings before dismissal occurs) it is a breach of contract if the procedure is not

123

observed. (Tomlinson v L.M.S Rly (1944). If the contract states that the dismissal may only occur for certain specified reasons, a dismissal is wrongful if the reason for the dismissal is other than specified in the contract.

However, it should be noted that the 2002 Employment Act introduced the obligation on an employer to include a statutory disciplinary and grievance procedure which must be in the contract or written terms and must be followed before any dismissal proceedings can take place.

Waiver of rights

If an employee's conduct justified a summary dismissal, the right must have been exercised within a reasonable time of the conduct, which allegedly justified the action since delay may amount to a waiver of the breach of contract.

Employee leaving

An employee is entitled to terminate employment at any time by giving the amount of notice required by the contract. If the employee is deemed to have been entitled to terminate employment by reason of the employer's conduct that may constitute a constructive dismissal and the fact that he gave notice makes no difference.

If an employer's attitude causes an employee to terminate his contract without notice, this may well constitute constructive dismissal and the employee may act accordingly.

Termination by agreement

The parties to a contract of employment as with any other contract, may terminate their relationship by agreement at any time upon such terms as they may agree, e.g. payment of money as a golden handshake. It should be noted that a termination by agreement is

124

not a dismissal for the purposes of the redundancy and unfair dismissals provisions of the 1996 Act. However, the tribunals are concerned to ensure that any alleged agreement to terminate a contract of employment is real and not merely a result of pressure imposed on an employee who is unaware of the significance of agreeing to terminate the contract and who faces dismissal as an alternative to so agreeing.

Termination by frustration

Frustration occurs whenever the law recognises that without default of either party a contractual obligation has become incapable of being performed because the circumstance in which performance would be called for would render it a thing different from that which was undertaken by the contract (Lord Radcliffe in Davis Contractors v Fareham UDC (1956)).

In the context of a contract of employment, the term frustration means that circumstances have arisen, without the fault of either party, that make it impossible for the contract to be performed in the way that may be reasonably expected and the contract automatically terminates without the need for notice to be given. Frustration of the contract is not deemed to be dismissal for legislative purposes. Examples of frustration may be sickness. In Notcutt v Universal Equipment Co (1986), a worker with 27 years service, who was two years from retirement suffered a permanently incapacitating heart attack. The court decided that this rendered performance of the contract impossible and therefore the contract was frustrated as he was unable to perform his obligation to work. The employee was therefore not entitled to sick pay during his period of notice.

Imprisonment is another example, however this has caused problems. In 1986, the Court of Appeal allowed a four year apprenticeship contract to be frustrated by a six months Borstal sentence: FC Shepherd LTD v Jerrom (1986). In this case court held that such a period of imprisonment made the performance of the contract impossible. As with the sickness, the courts will tend to look at each case on its own merits without applying hard and fast rules.

Action for wrongful dismissal

An employee who has been wrongfully dismissed may bring an action for damages against his former employer representing the amount of wages owed to him in respect of work already done and in respect of wages that the employee would have earned had he been given the amount of notice to which he was entitled. The amount of wages lost is determined by the ordinary principles of common law and includes all sums connected with the job, such as loss of tips etc. Damages for wrongful dismissal cannot normally include compensation for injured feelings or pride or the fact that future earnings may be affected.

The object of damages is to compensate the injured party for what he actually lost, not to punish the party in breach of contract, and therefore the courts have developed principles to ensure that the employee who has been wrongfully dismissed receives compensation only for his actual loss.

In the case of *Brighton & Sussex University Hospitals NHS Trust v Akinwunmi,* 2017, Mr Akinwunmi ('Mr A') was a consultant neurosurgeon for the NHS trust. Mr A had poor relationships with a number of fellow surgeons, and had previously complained that he was being bullied - and bought a race discrimination claim to the Employment Tribunal, which was settled. It had been agreed that Mr A would take an unpaid three month sabbatical. During this sabbatical, Mr A raised some concerns about patient safety and alleged that his colleagues were turning away NHS patients whilst accepting private work. His colleagues claimed that he was
126

incompetent and his practices were unsafe. A complaint was made to the police that Mr A had also threatened to assault one of his colleagues. The police decided to take no further action - but the Trust failed to notify Mr A of this.

A decision was made to limit his sabbatical to three months, Mr A appealed against this decision but his appeal was not upheld, and his absence from work became unauthorised. Mr A argued that it was impossible for him to return to work as there were various serious outstanding issues with his colleagues and this could be a risk to patient safety. Mr A was also concerned the police might arrest him if he returned to work and came into contact with the colleague he was alleged to have threatened.

The Trust stated that the complaints could not be dealt with *until* he returned. A disciplinary hearing was held and Mr A was dismissed because of his unauthorised absence. Mr A brought claims for unfair dismissal, automatic unfair dismissal because of whistleblowing and victimisation.

The ET dismissed Mr A's claims for whistleblowing and victimisation but did find that his dismissal was unfair. On appeal the Employment Appeal Tribunal agreed that dismissing Mr A for his unauthorised absence was unfair because the full context of the absence was not taken into consideration by the Trust. The EAT held it was unreasonable for the Trust to expect Mr A to return to work before trying to resolve the outstanding issues and improve working relationships. The EAT agreed that insisting Mr A return to a workplace where people's lives could depend on good working relationships was particularly unreasonable. The EAT noted that the Trust's witnesses were found to be 'disingenuous' when giving evidence.

Damages against employee

Where an employee fails to give sufficient notice to his employer, the employer may sue the employee for damages representing the loss, which follows from the breach of contract. In practice, such actions are infrequent because the loss is often minimal.

Specific performance

Specific performance is an order from the court directing that the parties to a contract perform their contractual obligations. It is a fundamental principle of labour law that specific performance is granted to compel performance of a contract of employment and this principle is now embodied in s 235 of the Trade Union and Labour Relations (Consolidation) Act 1992.

Injunction

An injunction is an order from a court forbidding certain conduct, e.g. the breaking of a term of the contract of employment. Hence it may be used to prevent a breach of a covenant restraining an employee from taking employment with a rival of his former employer. The courts usually refuse to grant an injunction if it compels performance.

By virtue of the Trade Union and Labour Relations Act 1992, no court may issue an injunction if the effect of such an order would be to compel an employee to do any work or to attend any place to work.

However, where the injunction compelling performance is to the benefit of the employee, the court may be prepared to grant such an order. In Hill v CA Parsons LTD (1972) the defendant employers wished to enter into an agreement with an organisation of workers whereby it was agreed that all employers in certain sections, including the plaintiff, would be obliged to join that organisation. This arrangement was legal at the time but under the Industrial Relations Act 1971 it would have been invalid. The plaintiff did not wish to join the organisation and he was dismissed with four weeks notice.

128

The Court of Appeal held that he was wrongfully dismissed since he was entitled to at least six months notice and furthermore an injunction was awarded which prevented the employee from being dismissed until that time elapsed by which time he would have a remedy under the 1971 Act.

Declaration

A declaration is an order from the court, which simply determines the rights of the parties in the case. It has no binding force in itself and is not available to all employees being restricted to those persons whose employment is derived from statute.

Written statement of reasons for dismissal

An employee who has been continuously employed for 2 years who has been dismissed, subject to the statutory provisions of the 2002 Act and the following of a formal procedure, is entitled to receive, upon request, a written statement of the reasons for his dismissal. The employer must supply the reason in writing within 14 days of the request. A claim may be presented to an industrial tribunal by an employee that his employer has "unreasonably" refused to provide a written statement of the reasons for dismissal or that it is inadequate or untrue. The right to a written statement only arises where the employee has been dismissed by his employer.

Suspension

In accordance with the general principle that an employer fulfils his contractual obligations by paying wages in accordance with the contract of employment, he may suspend an employee on full wages without breach of contract. An employer may only suspend an employee without pay if the contract expressly or impliedly provided for this. If the contract does not so provide, it is a breach of contract. Therefore, an employee who is suspended without contractual authority may treat himself as dismissed and claim accordingly.

Unfair Dismissal

The present law relating to unfair dismissal is to be found in the Employment Rights Act 1996. The significance of the concept of unfair dismissal is that it represents a further, and most important, step towards recognising the property right, which an employee has in his job. Additionally, it is no longer possible for an employer to end a contract by simply giving notice and thereby totally discharging his responsibilities. The threat of dismissal is no longer quite so important since the employee has a remedy if the threat is implemented. The 1996 Act provides that, subject to certain specified exceptions, every employee has the right not to be unfairly dismissed. It should be noted that a complaint of unfair dismissal does not depend upon the employer having acted in breach of contract but simply that the employer has terminated the contract in circumstances which are unfair. Certain categories of employees are excluded: employees who, at the effective date of termination of the contract have been continuously employed for less than one year, *two years if employed after 6th April 2012*, persons over retiring age, persons employed in the police service, share fishermen, employees who ordinarily work outside Great Britain, employees employed on fixed term contracts and persons covered by a designated dismissals procedure agreement.

Dismissal

If an action for unfair dismissal is to succeed, the employee must first establish that he was dismissed within the meaning of the Act. The employee must establish constructive dismissal if alleged.

The Act provides that:

"an employee shall be treated as dismissed by his employer if the contract under which he is employed by the employer is terminated by the employer whether it is so terminated by notice or without notice or where under that contract he is employed for a fixed term, that term expires without being renewed under the same contract or the employee terminates that contract, with or without notice, in circumstances such that he is entitled to terminate it without notice by reason of the employers conduct".

The Act refers to the concept of so-called "constructive' dismissal. If an employee leaves employment entirely voluntarily, there is no dismissal but if he leaves because of the employers conduct then it may be deemed "constructive"

The courts and tribunals have been concerned to define the circumstances in which an employee is entitled to regard himself as having been constructively dismissed. In Western Excavating LTD v Sharp (1978) the tribunals found that sufficiently unreasonable behaviour on the part of the employer entitled an employee to leave his job and claim constructive dismissal. However, the Court of Appeal rejected the unreasonableness test and established that the correct test is one based on strict contractual principles. Accordingly, an employee is only able successfully to argue constructive dismissal where the employer has breached the contract in such a way as to justify the employee in treating himself as discharged from further performance. The action of an employer may involve breach of an express or implied term.

When is dismissal unfair?

The expression "unfair dismissal" is in no sense a commonsense expression capable of being understood by the person in the street. Whether a dismissal is unfair is affected, but not conclusively determined, by whether one or both parties has broken the terms of the contract of employment. The employer cannot, in seeking to

131

show that a dismissal was not unfair rely on alleged misconduct not known to him at the time of the dismissal. An otherwise fair dismissal is not automatically rendered unfair by a failure to give proper notice.

Reasonableness. It is for the employer to establish the reason for the dismissal. The tribunal must then satisfy itself as to whether the employer acted reasonably or unreasonably. The EAT laid down the following general principles in Iceland Frozen Foods v Jones (1982):

a) In applying the provisions of the 1996 Act a tribunal must consider the reasonableness of the employers conduct and not simply whether they (the members of the tribunal) consider the dismissal unfair.

b) In judging the reasonableness of the employer's conduct a tribunal must not substitute its own decision as to what was the right course to adopt for that of the employer.

c) In many cases there is a band of reasonable responses to the employees conduct within which one employer might take one view and another quite reasonably another.

d) The function of the tribunal is to determine whether in the particular circumstances the decision to dismiss fell within the band of reasonable responses, which a reasonable employer might have adopted. If the dismissal falls within the band it is fair. If it falls outside the band it is unfair.

In deciding whether an employer acted reasonably, the industrial tribunal is required to have regard to the provisions of the ACAS Code of Practice-Disciplinary Code of Practice and Procedures in Employment. In broad terms, this provides that the disciplinary rules and procedures ought to have been made known to each employee and that a disciplinary procedure ought to contain certain essential procedures.

Reasons for dismissal

There are five categories of reasons, which, if one is established by the employer, may make the dismissal fair provided that the tribunal is satisfied that the employer acted reasonably. These are as follows:

a) Capability or qualification
b) Conduct
c) Redundancy
d) Illegality of continued employment
e) Some other substantial reason.

In addition, an employer in certain circumstances, can dismiss an employee for reasons connected to pregnancy. Usually, it is automatically unfair to do so unless the employer can establish that at the effective date of termination, because of her pregnancy, she:
a) is or will have become incapable of adequately doing the work she is employed to do or: or
b) cannot or will not be able to do the work she is employed to do without a contravention (either by her or her employer) of a duty of restriction imposed by law.

In Brown v Stockton on Tees Borough Council (1988) the House of Lords (Supreme Court) held that if a woman was selected for redundancy because she is pregnant, such a dismissal is automatically unfair. Indeed, Lord Griffith stated that "it surely cannot have been intended that an employer should be entitled to take advantage of a redundancy situation to weed out his pregnant employer".

However, even where the circumstances of a and b above apply, the dismissal is still unfair if the employer has a suitable vacancy, i.e. appropriate for a pregnant woman to do and not substantially

133

less favourable than her existing employment in relation to the nature, terms and place of employment, which he fails to offer her.

Another case highlighting unfair dismissal was that of Georgia O'Brian v Bolton St Catherine's Academy. Ms O'Brien's ordeal began in 2011 when she was assaulted by a pupil at Bolton St Catherine's Academy whilst assisting a colleague with a disruptive student. Her physical injuries were not long-lasting in comparison with her mental reaction, resulting in an absence from the school and subsequent termination of her employment in January 2013.

In March 2017, the Court of Appeal confirmed that the decision of the Employment Tribunal in November 2014 was correct and should stand. In 2014, the Employment Tribunal found that Ms O'Brien's condition amounted to a disability and that her termination of employment was discriminatory and unfair. The school went on to appeal the decision and in September 2015 the Employment Appeal Tribunal (EAT) allowed the school's appeal. However in March 2017, the Court of Appeal overturned the EATs decision.

Another interesting case was that of Michael Hayward v Chadwicks Butchers. Michael Hayward had worked for Noel Chadwick, described to Manchester Employment Tribunal as a small and well-respected butchers in Wigan, for seven and a half years before he was dismissed for recommending a discount from online retailer Fresh Meat Packs North West to his then-girlfriend on Facebook.

Hayward was subsequently dismissed for gross misconduct and breach of contract by father and son directors John and Paul Chadwick for 'advertising' what they believed to be a competitor and breaching the company's social media policy. The tribunal heard the pair, whose business did not have a formal HR function, had already decided to dismiss Hayward before they brought him into a disciplinary meeting in April 2016.

The 37-year-old said he was not issued a written or verbal formal warning, despite requesting one, nor was he given the opportunity to have someone with him at the meeting or given an explanation regarding his actions. As no appeal was arranged within a few weeks of his sacking, Hayward eventually lost confidence in Noel Chadwick and did not follow up the matter.

The tribunal also heard that Hayward had been 'pulled up' on his use of social media before he posted the offer, but there was no warning given to him that suggested such behaviour could lead to his dismissal.

Allowing Hayward's unfair dismissal claim, Judge Keith Robinson called Noel Chadwick "fanciful" for suggesting it experienced any financial or reputational loss because of the Facebook post.

"Hayward's misdemeanour, if one can call it that, was minor," the judge continued. "This is not an advertisement; this [matter] was a wholly mishandled dismissal root and branch. The claimant was dismissed summarily in a process that was reprehensible."

The judge awarded Hayward a £6,091 payout – £4,891 in lost wages and compensation, and £1,200 to reimburse his tribunal fees.

Three other recent interesting cases based around unfair dismissal are:

Genus and Kelly v Fortem Solutions Ltd 2018. Two repair contractors who were fired for gross misconduct after they were discovered to have used company vehicles for personal purposes were unfairly dismissed, While the pair were at fault for misusing the vans, the tribunal found their employer failed to thoroughly investigate the issue before dismissing them

Evans Nixon v Staffordshire South West Citixens Advice Bureau 2018 involved a long-standing CAB employee who had been dismissed for redundancy after a series of funding cuts. A selection exercise had been undertaken to determine who was made redundant, and the Claimant argued that she had been unfairly disadvantaged in the scoring process while less experienced colleagues had been retained. She also argued that her age and her disability (she suffers from a brain disorder called leukoencephalopathy) were factors in the CAB's decision to dismiss her.

The Employment Tribunal considered her case and found that the individual scores had not been discussed with her, and she also had not been given a chance to dispute the scores before the CAB had taken the decision to terminate her employment. On that basis, the Claimant's dismissal had been procedurally unfair. However, the Tribunal found that there was no disability or age discrimination.

Talon Engineering Ltd v Smith 2018. Mrs Smith worked for a motorcycle manufacturer, Talon Engineering Ltd, and sent an email to a company that Talon dealt with calling one of her colleagues an unpleasant name. Following an investigation in to her conduct, Mrs Smith was called to a disciplinary meeting but her Union rep was unable to attend on the allotted day. Several alternative dates were suggested by Mrs Smith and her rep, the first being 2 weeks ahead. Talon were not willing to delay the hearing to accommodate Mrs Smith's companion and so it went ahead in her absence. Mrs Smith was found to have committed gross misconduct and was summarily dismissed. She appealed and her appeal was rejected. Mrs Smith then brought a claim in the Employment Tribunal for unfair dismissal.

The Tribunal found that Talon had a potentially fair reason for dismissing Mrs Smith, i.e. conduct, but concluded that no reasonable employer would have refused a further short postponement of the disciplinary hearing and gone ahead in her absence. It was noted that the further delay to ensure Mrs Smith's attendance and grant her the opportunity to be heard and accompanied would have been a short one.

Talon appealed to the Employment Appeal Tribunal (EAT), however, the EAT upheld the finding of unfair dismissal. The EAT also considered the right to be accompanied under section 10 of the ERA 1996, which says that the employer must postpone the hearing to allow the employee's chosen companion to attend, if the proposed alternative is within 5 working days.

The EAT found that Talon appeared to believe that because Mrs Smith's union rep suggested dates which did *not* fall within 5 working days, they were not obliged to reschedule the hearing.

Dismissal for trade union reasons

References in this section are to the Trade Union and Labour Relations (Consolidation) Act 1992. Trade Union membership or activities. Except in exceptional cases, a dismissal is automatically unfair if the employee can establish that the principal reason for it was that the employer was, or proposed to become, a member of an independent trade union, or that the employee had taken or proposed to take part in the activities of an independent trade union at any appropriate time or that the employee was not a member of any or a particular trade union, or had refused or proposed to refuse to become or remain a member.

Other reasons for dismissal

An industrial tribunal cannot determine whether a dismissal was fair or unfair if it is known that at the date of dismissal the employer was conducting or instituting a lock out or the complainant was taking part in a strike or other industrial action, unless it is shown:

a) that one or more relevant employees of the same employer have not been dismissed: or

b) that any such employee has, before the expiry of the period of three months beginning with the employee's date of dismissal, been offered re-engagement and that the complainant has not been offered re-engagement.

National security

If an employee has shown to have been dismissed on grounds of national security, as evidenced by a certificate signed by or on behalf of a minister of the Crown, the tribunal must dismiss the complaint. In Council of Civil Service Unions v Minister for the Civil Service (1985) (the GCHQ case), the court held that the requirements of national security outweighed those of fairness when the minister decided to ban trade unions at GCHQ, without consultation with the trade unions. Workers who refused to give up their trade union membership were subsequently fairly dismissed.

Procedure

An employee who considers that he has been unfairly dismissed may present a complaint to the Central Office of Industrial Tribunals within three months of the effective date of termination or within such further period as the tribunal considers reasonable in a case where it is satisfied that it was not reasonably practicable for the complaint to be presented within a time period of three months. Where the dismissal is unfair (failure to offer re-engagement where the dismissal is connected with a lockout or strike) the time limit is six months from the date of dismissal. A copy of the application is sent to the employer as respondent. If the employer wishes to contest any aspect of the complaint, he must enter a "notice of appearance" within 14 days, although tribunals have a wide discretion to grant an extension of time. Once this has happened, a date is set down for the hearing of the case by an industrial tribunal.

Conciliation

A copy of the application is also sent to a conciliation officer. He is under a statutory duty, either at the request of the parties or on his own initiative, to endeavor to promote a voluntary settlement of the issue, either by way of an agreement to reinstate or re-engage the complainant or an agreement as to the payment of compensation in respect of the dismissal. there is no legal duty upon the parties to co-operate with the conciliation officer.

Pre-hearing Assessments

Under the Industrial Tribunals Regulations (S1 1985/16) provision is made for a pre-hearing assessment of the case to be made at the request of either of the parties or on the notion of the tribunal itself. At the tribunal, it is for the complainant to establish that he was dismissed (unless dismissal is conceded). It is then for the tribunal to satisfy itself as to whether the dismissal was fair or unfair in accordance with the principles stated above. If the dismissal is found to be unfair, the tribunal will consider the remedies, which may be awarded. An appeal, on a point of law only, lies from an industrial tribunal to the Employment Appeal Tribunal.

Remedies

Reinstatement and re-engagement orders. If the Tribunal finds the dismissal unfair, it must explain to the complainant the remedies available and ask if he wishes to be reinstated or re-engaged. If the employee indicates that this is his wish then the Tribunal must consider whether it is practicable for the employer to comply with such an order. If the employer complies, but not fully, with a reinstatement or re-engagement order then, unless the tribunal is satisfied that it was not practicable to comply with the order, an additional award of compensation must be made.

139

If a reinstatement or re-engagement order is made but not complied with at all or if no such order is made, the tribunal must make an award of compensation on the basis of the following:

a) basic award, amount of which is calculated in line with redundancy payments;

b) compensatory award, being an amount that the tribunal considers just and equitable in all the circumstances having regard to the loss suffered by the complainant in consequence of the dismissal in so far as the loss is attributable to action taken by the employer subject to a maximum limit.

****

Chapter 8

Discrimination in the Workplace

The ability of employers to discriminate in the workplace has been steadily eroded. In 2010, the Equality Act came onto the statute books and was implemented in two stages, October 2010 and April 2011. The Act replaced nine previous pieces of legislation, bringing them all under one umbrella.

The main changes contained within the Equality Act 2010 are making pay secrecy gagging clauses unenforceable, putting restrictions on employers asking job applicants questions about disability or health, making employers responsible for protecting their staff from harassment by customers and allowing employment tribunals that find an employer has discriminated against an employee to make recommendations that could affect the whole workforce.

The Equality Act replaced the Equal Pay Act 1970, The Sex Discrimination Act 1975, the Race Relations Act 1976, The Disability Discrimination Act 1996, The Employment Equality (Sexual Orientation) Regulations 2003, The Employment equality (Religion or Belief) Regulations 2003 and the Employment Equality (Age) Regulations 2006, the Equality Act 2006 and the Equality Act (Sexual Orientation) Regulations 2007. In most cases, the thrust of the Acts that were incorporated into the Equality Act 2010 have remained unchanged, but are now contained within the 2010 legislation.

Equal Pay

In broad terms, the Equal Pay Act 1970, which has now been replaced wholesale by the Equality Act 2010, was concerned with less favourable treatment of one person relative to another in respect of matters governed by the contract under which a person is employed whereas the Sex Discrimination act 1975 dealt with less favourable treatment in matters not governed by the contract, on grounds of sex and/or marital status.

The Equal Pay Act 1970 was influenced by the treaty of Rome and the effect of certain European Community Directives have been considerable in this area and have significant practical consequences for any applicant contemplating bringing an action alleging breach of the Equality Act 2010.

Article 119 of the Treaty of Rome provides that: "each member state shall maintain the application of the principle that men and women should receive equal pay for equal work. For the purpose of this article, pay means the ordinary basic or minimum wage or salary and any other consideration, whether in cash or kind, which the worker receives, directly or indirectly in respect of his employment from his employer. The Article is directly enforceable by individuals in the courts of member states of the EEC. The 2002 Employment Rights Act introduced the right of the employee to give the employer a questionnaire in order to ascertain whether or not the employer is actually paying and treating equally. The employer does not have to comply.

Sex Discrimination

The Equality Act 2010 makes it unlawful for an employer to discriminate against employees because of their sex. Sex discrimination against men is just as unlawful as sex discrimination against women. Also, it is unlawful for a woman to discriminate
142

against another woman because of her sex, and for a man to discriminate against another man because of his sex.

There are four main types of discrimination.

Direct discrimination

Is when someone is treated differently and not as well as other people because of their sex. For example, advertising a job and stating it is better suited to female applicants. It breaks down into three different sorts of treating someone 'less favourably' because of:

- their own sex (ordinary direct discrimination)
- their perceived sex (direct discrimination by perception)
- their association with someone of a particular sex (direct discrimination by association).

Indirect discrimination

Can occur where a workplace rule, practice or procedure is applied to all employees, but disadvantages those of a particular sex. For example, a requirement that job applicants must be six feet tall could be met by significantly fewer women than men.

An employee or job applicant claiming indirect discrimination must show how they have been personally disadvantaged, as well as how the discrimination has or would disadvantage other employees of the same sex.

In some limited circumstances, indirect discrimination may be justified in law if it is necessary for the business to work. However, employers should note this can be a difficult process.

Harassment

This breaks down into three different types:

143

- 'unwanted conduct' related to a person's sex causing a distressing, humiliating or offensive environment for them
- 'unwanted conduct' of a sexual nature - this is sexual harassment
- less favourable treatment of an employee because they have rejected sexual harassment or been the victim of it.

An interesting case in relation to Sexual harassment is that of Ms M Podlecka v MYM Global Ltd 2018 **where** the Employment Tribunal held that the Claimant should be awarded over £15,000 in compensation after she was wrongfully dismissed and discriminated against. Ms Podlecka commenced employment with MYM Global Ltd on 21 December 2016 as a Cost Estimator. Ms Podlecka alleged that he following had occurred during the course of her employment:

- That she had been subjected to sex discrimination in the workplace by Moshe Genish, the owner of the business and her line manager – comments of a sexualised nature were made by him and Mr Genish also inappropriately touched her hand on a few occasions;
- That her colleagues had acted in a hostile manner towards her;
- That Claudiu Praj had subjected her to abusive language and made derogatory comments about her religion and how old she was
- That Mr Praj would treat her as a secretary and not in the same way as he would treat male colleagues
- On 8 August 2017 Ms Podlecka complained to Mr Genish about Mr Praj's conduct. He launched an informal investigation; Ms Podlecka felt that the investigation did not include her enough and so she went home.

On 9 August 2017 Ms Podlecka sent Mr Genish an email containing a formal grievance (which complained primarily about Mr Praj's conduct). On 11 August 2017 Mr Genish dismissed Ms Podlecka, calling her immature and stating that the workplace was not a kindergarten. Ms Podlecka subsequently made Employment Tribunal claims for sex discrimination, unlawful deduction from wages, and notice pay.

The decision of the Employment Tribunal

The Employment Tribunal gave default judgment in Ms Podlecka's claims, MYM Global Ltd having failed to have provided a response to the claim. The Employment Tribunal awarded Ms Podlecka the following sums as compensation for her successful claims:

£10,000 in respect of injury to feelings (in compensation for the sex discrimination claim)
£1,750 in respect of loss of earnings
£350 in respect of notice pay
£1,250 in respect of holiday pay

An uplift of 25% for failure to comply with the ACAS Code of Practice.

Victimisation
Treating an employee unfairly who has made or supported a complaint about sex discrimination.

Other considerations

In very limited circumstances, there are some jobs which can require that the job-holder is a man or a woman. This is known as an 'occupational requirement'. One example is where the job holder is likely to work in circumstances where members of one sex are in

145

a state of undress and might reasonably object to the presence of a member of the opposite sex, such as in a bra-fitting service.

Making a claim of Sex discrimination

If an employee feels they been discriminated against, they will be able to bring a claim to an employment tribunal. However, as with all matters it's best they talk to their employer first to try to sort out the matter informally.

Sexual Orientation

The Equality Act 2010 makes it unlawful to discriminate against employees, job seekers and trainees because of their sexual orientation. For example, an employer not promoting an employee purely because they are gay is likely to be discrimination.

The Act defines Sexual orientation as:

- orientation towards people of the same sex (lesbians and gay men)
- orientation towards people of the opposite sex (heterosexual)
- orientation towards people of the same sex and the opposite sex (bisexual).

The law applies equally whether someone is a lesbian, gay man, heterosexual or bisexual.

There are four main types of sexual orientation discrimination.

Direct discrimination

Breaks down into three different sorts of direct discrimination of treating someone 'less favourably' because of:

- their actual sexual orientation (ordinary direct discrimination)
- their perceived sexual orientation (direct discrimination by perception)

146

- the sexual orientation of someone with whom they associate (direct discrimination by association).

Indirect discrimination

Can occur where there is a policy, practice, procedure or workplace rule which applies to all employees, but disadvantages people of a particular sexual orientation. An example of this could be a particular policy for maternity/paternity leave does not apply to same-sex couples. In some limited circumstances, indirect discrimination may be justified if it is what the law terms 'a proportionate means of achieving a legitimate aim'.

Harassment

When unwanted conduct related to sexual orientation has the purpose or effect of violating an individual's dignity or creating an intimidating, hostile, degrading, humiliating or offensive environment for that individual.

Victimisation

Is when an employee suffers what the law terms a 'detriment' - something that causes disadvantage, damage, harm or loss - because, for example, they have made or supported a complaint about sexual orientation discrimination.

'Coming out' at work

When someone tells other people about their sexual orientation this is known as 'coming out'. This process is personal and different for everyone. While many lesbian, gay and bisexual people are 'out' in their personal lives, they may not want to 'come out' at work.

If the employee is limiting who they tell, they also need to decide whether they want those people to keep the details of their sexual

147

orientation confidential. If someone reveals a person's sexual orientation to others against that person's will, this may be seen as:

- harassment and/or
- a breach of the Data Protection Act (if details are stored as confidential data) and/or
- a breach of any of the employer's relevant regulations or policies.

Harassment because of Sexual orientation

Harassment because of sexual orientation can take many different forms. It could be a verbal or written comment, what somebody thinks is a 'joke', exclusion from conversations or activities, violence or the threat of violence.

An employee's complaint of this nature should be taken seriously and the employer should take care to listen to their concerns. It should also be mindful that this type of complaint can be difficult for the individual to discuss.

It is important for an employer to deal with this type of complaint, not only because of its legal obligations, but also because there could be knock-on effects. The employee being harassed might feel de-motivated and their productivity fall, or it might lead to them being absent from work through stress. A climate of harassment can also damage morale in the workplace.

An employer may benefit from having a specific policy setting out how it would deal with complaints about sexual orientation discrimination.

Sexual orientation and Religion or belief

The Equality Act has specific exemptions where employment is for the purpose of organised religion, such as being a Minister or otherwise promoting or representing the religion.

This means that some roles can be restricted to people of a particular sexual orientation. There can also be additional requirements related to sexual orientation, such as a requirement for gay men or lesbians to be celibate. Restrictions concerning religion can also apply to the protected characteristics of sex, gender reassignment, and marriage and civil partnership. Such a restriction only applies when:

- appointing a person who meets the requirement/s in question is a proportionate way of complying with the doctrines of the religion, or
- because of the nature or context of the employment, employing a person who does not meet the requirement/s would conflict with a significant number of the religion's followers' strongly-held religious convictions. The requirement/s must be a proportionate way of avoiding such a conflict.

Making a claim of Sexual orientation discrimination

If an employee feels they have been discriminated against, they may be able to make a claim to an employment tribunal. However, it's best to talk to the employer first to try to sort out the matter informally, in order to minimise the negative effects on all parties involved.

Race Relations

The Equality Act 2010 makes it unlawful to discriminate against employees, job seekers and trainees because of race - this includes the different elements of colour, nationality, and ethnic or national origin. For example, this would include turning down the best applicant for a job because they are Nigerian and the employer feels they would not 'fit in' with the rest of the staff because they are all English

.

There are four main types of race discrimination.

Direct discrimination

Breaks down into three different sorts of direct discrimination of treating someone 'less favourably' because of:

- their actual race (direct discrimination)
- their perceived race (direct discrimination by perception)
- the race of someone with whom they associate (direct discrimination by association).

Indirect discrimination

Can occur where there is a policy, practice, procedure or workplace rule which applies to all workers, but particularly disadvantages people of a particular race. For example, a requirement for all job applicants to have GCSE Maths and English would discriminate against potential candidates educated in countries which don't have GCSEs, unless the employer accepted equivalent qualifications.

In some limited circumstances, indirect discrimination may be justified if it is what the law terms 'a proportionate means of achieving a legitimate aim'.

Harassment

When unwanted conduct related to race has the purpose or effect of violating an individual's dignity or creating an intimidating, hostile, degrading, humiliating or offensive environment for that individual.

Victimisation

Unfair treatment of an employee who has made or supported a complaint about race discrimination.

Managing cultural differences at work

Employers and employees should be mindful that employees/colleagues will often come from different backgrounds, and aware that there may be cultural differences as a result, particularly regarding customs and values. They should be sensitive and respectful towards such differences. It is good practice for an employer to provide training for staff to establish a culture of respect in this area, and provide an understanding of what constitutes acceptable and unacceptable behaviours.

Managing languages at work

The increased movement of people around the world means it can be quite common for organisations to employ staff from many different countries or ethnic backgrounds. As a result, there may be employees for whom English is not their first language. Often, there may be a number of employees who originate from the same country or share a common language which is not English. However, an employer:

- can specify a language of operation, usually English, for business reasons. However, in Wales some jobs require the holder to speak both English and Welsh
- can insist on recruiting a job candidate who has skills in English necessary for the job, but it must not select based on assumptions about race, nationality, or ethnic or national origins. Again, in Wales some jobs require the holder to have skills in both English and Welsh necessary for the job
- should be wary of prohibiting or limiting the use of other languages within the workplace unless they can justify this with a genuine business reason.

Employing staff from abroad

As discussed in chapter 1, employers must check their employees are entitled to work in the UK, and should also ensure any necessary paperwork is correct and up to date. However, employers should ensure they are consistent in the checks they carry out. For

151

example, just doing them for potential new recruits they assume are not British citizens, or not from the Channel Islands, the Isle of Man or Republic of Ireland, may be potentially discriminatory. Workers from European Union countries plus Switzerland, Iceland, Liechtenstein and Norway are also entitled to work in the UK.

Ethnic and national origins and religion
Employers and employees should also be mindful that some ethnic and national groups have devout religious beliefs. For example, Sikhs have their own religion and the majority of Poles are Catholic. It is unlawful to discriminate against employees because of their religion or belief, or lack of religion or belief.

Making a claim of race discrimination
If someone feels they have been discriminated against, they may be able to make a claim to an employment tribunal. However, it's best to talk to the employer first to try to sort out the matter informally, in order to minimise the negative effects on all parties involved.

Discrimination on the grounds of disability
The 2010 Equality Act covers Discrimination on the grounds of disability. It is against the law for an employer:
- to treat a person less favourably because they are disabled than someone without a disability would be treated in the same circumstances. This is called direct discrimination
- to discriminate against a person because of their connection with someone else who is disabled, for example, their partner or child. This is called discrimination by association
- to discriminate against a person indirectly for example by requiring something which applies to all their colleagues but which is much more difficult for them and for disabled people to meet

- to treat a person unfavourably because of something connected with their disability. For example, a worker is given night shifts to do. They have kidney failure and has nightly dialysis. Making them do night shifts would mean they wouldn't be able to have their dialysis
- not to make reasonable adjustments to the workplace to allow a person to work or to continue to work
- to harass a person if they are disabled, for example, by making jokes about their disability
- to victimise a person if they take legal action because of discrimination against them, or if they help someone else to take legal action because of discrimination

Employers can treat disabled people less favourably only if they have a sufficiently justifiable reason for doing so, and only if the problem cannot be overcome by making 'reasonable adjustments'. For example, an employer would be justified in rejecting someone with severe back pain for a job as a carpet fitter, as they cannot carry out the essential requirements of the job.

Examples of the types of adjustments that an employer might make include:

- making physical adjustments to the premises
- supplying special equipment to help a person do their job, or providing information in an accessible format
- transferring a person to a different post or workplace
- altering hours of work or giving extra time off

When employers are deciding whether an adjustment is reasonable they can take into account several things, including the cost of making an adjustment and the size of their business. If a person is already in the job, their employer can also take into account their skills and experience and the length of time they have worked there.

An interesting case relating to discrimination on the grounds of disability is Peninsula Business Systems v Baker 2017. In this recent case, the Claimant, Miss Baker, claimed that she suffered from Dyslexia. This was confirmed by a psychologist's report.

The Respondent, Peninsula, were concerned about the Claimant's performance and instructed consultants to conduct surveillance of her movements.

Miss Baker complained to an Employment Tribunal that the surveillance constituted harassment on the grounds of disability. Although the Employment Tribunal found in favour of the Claimant, it acknowledged that it had not been asked to determine the question of disability. The EAT, on appeal, confirmed that the protection of the discrimination legislation was not available to those who merely asserted a disability. It must be proven that the individual in question actually has a disability, are associated with a disabled person, or are wrongly perceived to be a disabled person.

Age discrimination in the workplace
On 1st October 2006, The Employment Equality (Age) Regulations (EE(A) Regs) took effect, outlawing age discrimination in both the workplace and vocational training. These Regulations have now been replaced wholesale by the Equality Act 2010. It is against the law to treat a person unfairly at work because of age. It is against the law to discriminate for being too young or old. The law only covers work, adult education and training. The law applies to a person whether working or applying for a job. It is against the law to bully or make offensive comments in the workplace because of age.

There are some exceptions to the general rule. For example, an employer may occasionally be allowed to discriminate against
154

someone because of their age but only if they can show that this is justified. An employer may argue that it doesn't make business sense to employ someone over 60 years of age if there is a long and involved period of training allied to the job.

There are several cases of note here. the first was the recent case of Gomes v Henworth Ltd, a Winkworth estate agency at the Watford EAT June 2017. A woman who was told she might be "better suited to a traditional estate agency" was discriminated against because of her age, the tribunal ruled. Ms Gomes, who was 59 when the comment was made, started working for Henworth, which traded as Winkworth Estate Agents, in February 2015 as an administrative assistant. She had worked for another agent in the Winkworth franchise since February 2009 before being transferred.

In February 2016, the company's lettings director had a meeting with Gomes to discuss her work, in which he told her she needed to be more careful with her work. This upset Gomes so she spoke to her line manager who, in turn, spoke to Graham Gold, one of the directors.

In March 2016, Gold asked Gomes to meet with him and told her: "This marriage isn't working." When she asked what this meant, Gold mentioned a letter had been typed and sent to a solicitor with errors, including referring to the solicitor as a deceased client's son and referring to the deceased as 'Mrs' rather than 'Mr', and a note would be placed on her performance record.

Gold then said she would be "better suited to a traditional estate agency", which Gomes claimed she took to mean he thought she was too old to work in that particular office.

Allowing Gomes' claim for age discrimination, the tribunal concluded the phrase 'better suited to a traditional estate agency' was a reference to her age, noting that it was defined in the Oxford English Dictionary as 'long established' and it was unlikely that such a comment would have been made to a younger employee. The tribunal also allowed the claims for harassment related to age and constructive unfair dismissal.

Another case of note, relating to sex discrimination and other factors was the long running case of BAE systems v Marion Konczak wghich ran from 2006 until it was decided in 2017 by the court of appeal.

Mrs Konczak was a secretary at BAE from 1998 until her dismissal in 2007. She experienced a series of stressful events. In April 2006, after a particularly difficult meeting, her line manager said that women take things more emotionally than men, who tend to forget things and move on. That comment, described in the judgment as the "Dent comment", was the final straw for Mrs Konczak, who did not return to work due to work-related stress.

The Employment Tribunal held that the Dent comment was an act of sex discrimination. It also upheld several other complaints, including of discriminatory dismissal in 2007, but the Dent comment was the important finding for the purposes of the Court of Appeal's decision. Following prolonged proceedings, in October 2014 the Employment Tribunal held that the Dent comment had caused Mrs Konczak's illness and that BAE was liable for all losses flowing from it, amounting to around £360,000. BAE argued on appeal that it was wrong in principle for it to be liable for such a large amount, especially given the various other events, for which it was not legally liable, which it said had contributed to Mrs Konczak's illness. It argued that the correct approach was for the tribunal to apportion liability between the different factors, following the decision of the EAT in *Thaine v London School of Economics* [2010] UKEAT 0144/10, [2010] ICR 1422. The Court of Appeal thought differently and BAE lost the case.

Retirement and age discrimination

The normal retirement age for both men and women is 65, unless
156

the employment contract states that it is higher. An employer was allowed to force a person to retire at the normal retirement age.

However, with the scrapping of the Default Retirement Age between April and October 2011, employers are no longer be able to force employees to retire at 65.

Unfair dismissal
It is discriminatory to dismiss a person because of age. A claim for unfair dismissal may be made if this has been the case.

****

Chapter 9

Being Made Redundant

Compensation for redundancy was one of the first employment protection rights introduced into our law. The first piece of legislation was the Redundancy Payments Act 1965 and the law is now contained in the main in the Employment Rights Act 1996 s 139. In addition, the Equality Act 2010 now has a bearing (see below).

In order to claim a redundancy payment an employee must have two years continuous service and be dismissed for reasons of redundancy. The definition of dismissal for redundancy purposes is contained within s 136 of the Employment Rights Act 1996.

These situations are the same as unfair dismissal that is, employer termination with or without notice, a fixed term contract expiring and constructive dismissal In addition, by s 139(4), if the employment is terminated by the death, dissolution or liquidation of the employer, or the appointment of a receiver, there is dismissal for reasons of redundancy.

The definition of redundancy is found in s 139(1) of the Act. This states that a redundancy has occurred if the dismissal is wholly or mainly attributable to:

a) the fact that his employer has ceased or intends to cease, to carry on the business for the purposes for which the employee was employed by him, or has ceased, or intends to cease, to carry on that business in the place where the employee was so employed or...
b) the fact that the requirements of that business for employees to carry out work of a particular kind, or for employees to carry out

158

work of a particular kind in the place where he was so employed, have ceased or diminished or are expected to cease or diminish. This means that the redundancy occurs in three situations - the employer increasing business the employee moving his place of business or the employer reducing his labour force.

One key case dealing with redundancy was that of Murray v Foyle Meats Ltd (1999) IRLR 562. The House of Lords (Supreme Court) held that the definition of redundancy requires two factual questions to be answered. These are: have the requirements of the employer's business for employees to carry out work of a particular kind ceased or diminished, or were they expected to cease or diminish? Was the dismissal of the employee attributable, wholly or mainly, to this state of affairs? This means looking at the employer's overall requirements to decide whether there has been a reduced need for employees irrespective of the terms of the individual's contract or of the function that each performed.

Consultation

An important requirement in redundancy situations is the need for consultation. Consultation may be directly with the employees concerned or with their representatives. It should be observed that while the size of an undertaking might affect the nature or formality of the consultation, it cannot excuse lack of consultation at all.

There is no legal maximum time period for consultation but there is a legal minimum as follows:

- Less than 20 redundancies - there are no set rules but guidelines set down for individual consultations must be followed.

- 20 or more redundancies - Collective redundancy formal procedures to be followed.
- 20-99 redundancies-the consultation must start at least 30 days before any dismissals take effect.
- 100 or more redundancies-the consultation must start at least 45 days before any dismissals take effect.

Failure to consult the employee about his redundancy may render the dismissal unfair. Unions must be consulted too. Where the employer has broken his statutory duty to consult, the union or employee representatives can apply to a tribunal for a protective award which is payable to those employees in respect of whom the representatives should have been consulted. Similar provisions relate to consultation where there is a transfer of an undertaking under the Transfer of Undertakings Regulations 1981. Where such a transfer takes place, Regulation 10 creates a duty on both the transferor and the transferee to inform the representatives. The remedy for failure to comply with the consultation provisions under the regulations is found in Regulation 11. The employer can raise the defence of special; circumstances. The maximum award which can be made under the Regulations is four weeks pay. This is set off against any protective award given to the employee. Since 1993, the duty on the tribunal to offset this payment against wages or payment in lieu of notice is removed.

A key case dealing with consultation and redundancy is that of Mugford v Midland Bank plc (1977) IRLR 208. In this case, the EAT held that a dismissal on the grounds of redundancy was not unfair because no consultation had taken place with the employee individually, only the recognized trade union. The EAT described the position with regard to consultation as follows: where no consultation about redundancy has taken place with either the trade union or the employee, the dismissal will normally be unfair,

160

unless the reasonable employer would have concluded that the consultation would be an utterly futile exercise; consultation with the trade union over the selection criteria does not of itself release the employer from considering with the employee individually his or her being identified for redundancy; it will be a question of fact and degree for a tribunal to consider whether the consultation with the individual and/or the trade union was so inadequate as to render the dismissal unfair.

According to King v Eaton Ltd (1996) consultation must be fair and proper, which means that there must be:

- Consultation when the proposals are still at a formative stage
- Adequate information and adequate time to respond
- A conscientious consideration by the employer of the response to consultation.

Consultation about collective redundancies

The provisions of the European Council Directive 98/59/EC on the approximation of the laws of Member states relating to collective redundancies (the Collective Redundancies Directive) are now contained in Pt 1V, Ch 11 TULCRA which outlines the procedure for handling collective redundancies. For these purposes, s 195(1) TULCRA defines a redundancy dismissal as 'for a reason not related to the individual concerned or for a number of reasons all of which are not so related'.

The consultation should be about ways of avoiding the dismissals, reducing the number of employees to be dismissed, and mitigating the circumstances of the dismissals. It is necessary for the employer to consult on each of these three aspects and not just on some of them. There is an obligation for the employer to undertake such consultations with a view to reaching agreement with the appropriate representatives. The employer must disclose the following information in writing to these representatives:

1. The reason for the proposal;
2. The numbers and descriptions of employees whom it is proposed to dismiss;
3. The total number of employees of any description employed by the employer at the establishment;
4. The proposed method of selecting those to be dismissed;
5. The proposed method of calculating payments if different from those required by statute; and
6. The number of agency works working temporarily for and under the supervision and direction of the employer; the parts of the employers undertaking in which they are engaged and the types of work they are carrying out.

Special circumstances

There are two 'escape' clauses for employers unable to comply with their obligations under s 188 TULCRA 1992:

1. Where there are special circumstances which make it not reasonably practicable for an employer to comply with the consultation and information requirements they are to take all steps towards compliance that are reasonably practicable in the circumstances;
2. Where they have invited affected employees to elect representatives and the employees have failed to do so within a reasonable time, then the employer must give all the affected employees the information set out above.

One key case outlining special circumstances is that of the Bakers Union v Clarke of Hove Ltd (1978) IRLR 366. The court held that there were three stages to deciding whether there was a defence in

162

any particular case. First, were there special circumstances? Second, did they render compliance with the statute not reasonably practicable? Third, did the employer take all the reasonable steps towards compliance as were reasonably practicable in the circumstances? In this case, insolvency was not special enough in itself to provide a defence.

Special circumstances mean something out of the ordinary or something that is not common. In any complaint to the Employment Tribunal the onus is on the employer to show that there were special circumstances.

Misconduct and redundancy

Section 140(1) of the Employment Rights Act 1996 provides that in certain situations the employee will be disentitled to a redundancy payment. This occurs when the employee terminates the contract where:

a) the employee commits an act of misconduct and the employer dismisses without notice or

b) the employee commits an act of misconduct and the employer dismisses with shorter notice than the redundancy notice or

(c) the employer, when the redundancy notice expires, gives the employee a statement in writing that the employer is entitled, by virtue of the employee's conduct, to dismiss without notice.

There are two exceptions to this. By s 140 (2) where an employee, while under notice of redundancy, takes part in a strike or other industrial action to protest against the redundancies. If however, an employee who is on strike is selected for redundancy, the tribunal will have no jurisdiction to hear the case unless there are selective dismissals (Simmons v Hoover (1977)).

By S 143 the employer can extend the redundancy notice period and require the employees to work in order to make up the days

163

lost by the industrial action and if the employees lose they disentitle themselves to a redundancy payment.

Suitable alternative employment

If the employer offers the employee his old job back or a different job which is suitable alternative employment, the new contact starts on the termination of the old or within four weeks of the old contract expiring and the employee unreasonably refuses the offer he is disentitled to a redundancy payment by virtue of sections 141(2) and (3). The section therefore means that two questions must be asked: is the offer suitable alternative employment and is the employee's refusal of that offer reasonable.

Trial period in new employment

If the terms of the new contract differ (wholly or in part) from the old contract, then by s 138 the employee is entitled to a trial period. By subsection (3) the statutory trial period is four weeks, but this can be extended by the employees contract as long as the period is in writing and specified precisely. If the employee is dismissed during the trial period, he is treated as being dismissed for the reason his original contract ended, that is, redundancy, and on the date his original contract ended, so entitling him to claim a redundancy payment. If the employee resigns, he is treated as dismissed for redundancy, unless his resignation was unreasonable.

Lay off and Short time working

In order to prevent redundancies, the employer may temporarily lay off his workers to put them on short time. By s 147 a lay off is where no work or pay is provided by the employer. Short time working is where less than half a weeks pay is earned. By s 148 where the lay off or short time has lasted for more than four consecutive weeks or six weeks in any thirteen, the employee can
164

give notice to his employer that he intends to claim a redundancy payment. He must give the notice in writing. The employer has a defense if he can show that he reasonably expects to provide full time work for the next thirteen weeks and he raises this defense in written counter notice served within seven days of receipt of the employee's intention to claim.

Redundancy compensation

A redundancy payment is calculated in the same way as the basic award for unfair dismissal and is therefore based on age and years of service. However, unlike the basic award, periods of employment below the age of 18 do not count and the employees period of continuity is deemed to start at his 18th birthday. (Employment Rights Act 1996 s 211(2)). Again, unlike the basic award there is no deduction for contributory conduct, but like the basic award, there will be no reduction for each month the employee works in the year before he attains the normal retirement age for the job, so that on reaching the age, or 65, whichever is lower, entitlement to a redundancy payment ceases.

If the redundancy is caused by the employer's insolvency, the employee may make a claim for a redundancy payment to the Department of Employment under s 166 of the Employment Rights Act 1996. While the Employee ranks as a preferential creditor in his employer's insolvency, this will not be much use if the employer has no assets and therefore additionally the Department can pay certain sums to the employee from the National Insurance Fund. This can be up to eight weeks wages, up to six weeks holiday pay, a basic award and other payments.

A person will normally be entitled to statutory redundancy pay if they are an employee and have been working for their current employer for 2 years or more. The entitlement is:

* half a week's pay for each full year under 22 years of age

- one week's pay for each full year over 22 or older, but under 41
- one and half week's pay for each full year over 41 or older

Length of service is capped at 20 years.

If a person was made redundant on or after 6 April 2018, their weekly pay is capped at £508 and the maximum statutory redundancy pay they can get is £15,240. If they were made redundant before 6 April 2018, these amounts will be lower.

There is a ceiling of 20 years worth of redundancy pay. Redundancy pay (including any severance pay) under £30,000 is not taxable.

Exceptions

A person is not entitled to statutory redundancy pay if:

- their employer offers to keep them on
- their employer offers them suitable alternative work which they refuse without good reason

Being dismissed for misconduct doesn't count as redundancy, so a person wouldn't get redundancy pay if this happened. they would not be entitled to statutory redundancy pay if they fall into one or more of the following categories:

- merchant seamen, former registered dock workers (covered by other arrangements) or share fishermen
- crown servants, members of the armed forces or police services
- apprentices who are not employees at the end of their training

- a domestic servant who is a member of the employer's immediate family

Transfers of Undertakings

The Transfer of Undertakings (Protection of Employment Regulations)) (TUPE) 2006 completely replaced the 1981 TUPE Regulations governing transfer of employment from one employer to another when a company/organization is merged/sold with or to another.

A transfer of undertaking is defined, in TUPE 2006 reg. 3(1) as being 'the transfer of an economic entity which retains its identity'. Reg 3.(2) goes on to define an economic entity. Regulation 4 provides that, on transfer the contracts of employment of employees of the transferor are automatically transferred to the transferee. The transferee takes over all the rights and liabilities of the contracts of employment except for the occupational pension scheme (reg 10). There is another important provision in regulation 7 which states that dismissal of an employee either before or after a transfer will be automatically unfair if sole or principal reason for the dismissal is either the transfer itself or a reason connected with the transfer which is not an economic, technical or organizational reason entailing changes in the workforce.

Further changes to TUPE in 2014

The TUPE Regulations are amended by the Collective Redundancies and Transfer of Undertakings (Protection of Employment) (Amendment) Regulations 2014), which came into force on 31 January 2014. These amendments do not extend to Northern Ireland and will apply in respect of transfers which take place on or after 31 January 2014.

Summary of changes

Under the new regulations:

Businesses will now be able to renegotiate terms and conditions in collective agreements 1 year after a transfer has taken place, provided that the overall change is no less favourable. Micro businesses will be able to inform and consult employees directly when there are no existing appropriate representatives. Under existing TUPE regulations businesses usually have to inform, and sometimes also consult, employee representatives such as trade unions representatives; for micro businesses with 10 or fewer employees, there are often no representatives which means that they have to be specifically elected for this purpose; this change will make this process much less bureaucratic

The new employer will be able to engage in pre-redundancy consultation with employees, with the consent of the old employer. Contractual changes will be permitted for economic, technical or organisational reasons with the agreement of the employee and or where a contractual right of variation exists

The regulations also clarify the existing law in a number of areas: in cases where employees' terms and conditions are provided for in collective agreements, only the terms and conditions in the collective agreements that are in place before the date of transfer will apply; any future changes will not bind the new employer, unless it has taken part in the bargaining process that brought about the changes.

The test for service provision changes will make clear that activities carried out after the change in provider must be fundamentally the same as those carried out by the previous person who has ceased to carry them out; this means that if businesses radically change the way they provide services, that change is unlikely to be subject to the TUPE regulations

Redundancy and the Equality Act 2010

The Equality Act 2010 now affects all areas of work, including redundancy. An employer cannot select a person for redundancy just because they are disabled. The criteria used to select people for redundancy must not put disabled people at a disadvantage unless there is a fair and balanced reason for doing this. The employer must make reasonable adjustments to any criteria used to select employees for redundancies. For more information on the Equality Act 2010 you should go to the Equality and Human Rights Commission website:

www.equalityhumanrights.com.

****

Chapter 10

Health and Safety at Work

The Health and Safety at Work Act 1974.

Although not seen as implied duties in the contract of employment, it would be incomplete to talk about the employer's liability in relation to the safety of his employees without a brief overview of the statutory provisions.

The 1974 Act was introduced as a result of the Robens Committee report of 1972. The Committee found that the law on health and safety was piecemeal and badly structured, with eleven pieces of major legislation supplemented by over 500 supplementary statutory provisions. The majority of the law based liability on occupation of premises. The Committee proposed a unification of the law, basing liability on employment not occupation of premises.

The Committees findings were embodied in the Health and Safety at Work Act 1974. The aim of the Act is twofold - to lay down general duties across the whole area of employment, and to provide a unified system of enforcement under the control of the Health and Safety Executive and local authorities. General duties are imposed upon various types of people, for example employers, suppliers and manufacturers, with the aim of ensuring a safe working environment.

Section 2(1) lays down the general duty on employers: "It shall be the duty of every employer to ensure, so far as is reasonably practicable, the health, safety and welfare of all his employees. This is further specified by subsection (2). The phrase to which all these
170

duties are subject is "so far as is reasonably practicable". The basis of the duties under s 2(2) is that of employment - it covers duties owed by n employer to his employees; the duties, however, extend beyond the employment relationship. Section 3(1) provides that employers should conduct their business in such a way, "in so far as is reasonably practicable to protect persons other than their own employees from risks to their health and safety.

Liability is imposed not only on those who physically occupy premises but also on those who are responsible for the maintenance of such premises, or the access to and exit from the premises. In addition, liability is imposed against those responsible for safety and absence of risk concerning plant or substances used on the premises.

Protection of those other than employees is continued in s 5. This imposes a duty on those who control work premises to use the best means practicable to prevent the emission of offensive or noxious substances and to render harmless any such substances, which are so emitted. This general duty overlaps with the more specific duties laid down in the Control of Pollution Act 1974.

The Act attempts to increase protection by imposing duties on designers, manufacturers, importers and suppliers. A chain of responsibility is therefore imposed from the design and manufacture of an article to its installation, use and maintenance. It can be seen, however, that the duties under the Act overlap and this demonstrates the stated aim of the legislation of accident prevention.

The duty owed to employees in that by s 2 of the Act, if the Employer employs five or more persons he should have a general policy on health and safety and bring this policy to the notice of his employees. The policy should identify who is responsible for health and safety and should point out particular health and safety problems and arrangements for dealing with them. The policy should also cover such matters as training and supervision, inspection procedures, safety precautions and consultative arrangements. In addition, it must tell the employee how he can complain about any health and safety risk to which he feels he is being exposed.

While the common law imposes no duty on the employee to look after his own health and safety, failure to do so could mean that any damages could be wiped out by the employer raising the defence of contributory negligence. given that the aim of the statutory duty is not to provide compensation, the Act places a duty on the individual employee to have regard to his own safety and that of those around him. Often, employers will make breach of health and safety regulations a disciplinary offence and in some case it may be fair to dismiss an employee for such a breach. In Rogers v Wicks and Wilson COIT 90/97 willful breach of a no smoking policy imposed for safety reasons was held to be a justifiable reason for dismissal.

Health and Safety Representatives

There is a right under the HSAW for employees to have a safety representative who will in turn report to the employer. Further regulations were introduced and under the Safety Representatives and Safety Committees Regulations 1977, safety representatives should investigate potential hazards and dangerous occurrences at the workplace, investigate complaints from employees relating to health and safety and make representations on these matters to the employer and to the health and safety inspectors. If two safety representatives so request in writing, the employer must establish a safety committee which can keep policy and practice under review.

Under the Health and Safety (Consultation with Employees) regulations 1996, employers must consult with employees either
172

directly or else with their elected representatives over the introduction of any measure or new technology which might affect health and safety, appointments under the Management of Health and Safety at Work Regulations 1999 and health and safety information generally. Health and safety representatives are entitled to time off in pursuit of their work.

Health and Safety Regulations and Codes of Practice

The Secretary of State has the power to make regulations, either on the proposal of the Health and Safety Commission or after consultation with it (HSWA s.15). The most important regulations are the Control of Substances Hazardous to Health Regulations 2002 (COSHH), but other examples include the Health and safety Information for Employees Regulations 1989 and the Noise at Work Regulations 1989.

Currently, consultation is taking place between the government and different agencies concerning the simplification of Health and Safety Regulations. For an in depth view of current health and safety regulations, which are many and varied, you should go to the Governments Health and Safety website www.hse.gov.uk.

****

Chapter 11

The Role of Trade Unions

Definition of a trade union

The statutory definition of a trade union is now found in s1 (a) of the Trade Union and Labour Relations (Consolidation) Act 1992 that provides that a trade union means:

"an organisation (whether temporary or permanent) which consists wholly or mainly of workers of one or more descriptions and whose principle purposes includes the regulations of relations between workers of that description or those descriptions and employers or employers associations."

The definition is wide and concentrates on the purpose of that body. Thus a body which had a subsidiary purpose of regulating relations between workers and employers would not be a trade union.

In the United Kingdom, there is a general freedom to associate, with the exception of the police and the armed forces. The freedom to form and belong to an association, whatever association, is regarded as a fundamental human right. However, as we all know, the history of relations between state and unions, employer and unions has always been fraught with problems.

Most employees (and employers) will be represented by some sort of trade union. Whether or not the trade union is active in the workplace or whether the individual is a member of the relevant trade union is another matter. The 2004 Employment Relations Act is the most significant legislation governing relations between employers/employees and Trade Unions. This has also been supplemented by the Information and Consultation of Employees (ICE) Regulations 2004 (more below). However, the Trade Union Act 2016 has now been passed (May 2016) which brings in significant new regulations affecting trade union activity.

The Trade Union Act 2016

The Trade Union Act 2016 was passed in May 2016. It was partly designed to address the perception that disruptive strikes were being called by unions despite low levels of support from members – especially in transport and other public services.

Regulations implementing central parts of the Act came into force on 1 March 2017, and accompanying updated codes of practice and guidance are also being rolled out. This area does not stand still. There are already calls in Parliament and the Greater London Authority to make a union's right to strike in transport and public services subject to a judge giving permission for it to proceed.

Information, notifications and expiry of the ballot mandate

Content of the ballot paper. The new rules require unions to include more detailed information on the ballot paper sent to members. This must now summarise the dispute in enough detail that members can understand what issues are unresolved, the action planned, and the period during which it is expected to take place. Any ballot sent to union members from 1 March 2017 must meet the requirements.

As unions are required to supply any affected employer with a copy of the ballot paper in advance, employers will be able to check the appropriate information is now included.

There are some interesting practical questions arising from these changes. For example, the duty to provide information about the nature of action short of a strike only relates to the voting paper. There is no similar change to the duty to give notice of the industrial action to the employer.

This means that if a union were to change its mind about the action, short of a strike, or indeed wanted to escalate the action short of a strike (for example from a "withdrawal of cooperation" to an overtime ban), it apparently has no duty to inform the employer of this. This seems to run contrary to the aim of this part of the Act which is to ensure the balloted employees and employer know what the dispute is about, exactly what action is being called for and when it will take place.

Information on outcome of the ballot. Unions must now inform all eligible voters of the result of the ballot (as well as the employer). All eligible voters must be informed of the following:

- The number of individuals that are entitled to vote in the ballot.
- The total number of votes cast.
- The number of individuals answering "Yes" and "No" to each question.
- The number of spoiled, or otherwise invalid ballots.
- Whether or not the number of votes cast is at least 50% of the number entitled to vote.
- Where the important public services provision applies (see below), whether the number of "Yes" votes cast is at least 40% of those entitled to vote.

Notice of planned action. Where a union gives notice to an employer that industrial action is to take place, the required notice

177

period is now extended to 14 days (or seven if agreed by union and employer).

Expiry of ballot authorisation. From 1 March, the authorisation for industrial action given by a "Yes" vote will have an expiry date. After six months from the date of the ballot (or up to nine months if agreed by union and employer) unions will have to re-ballot members to stage further action.

So, if voting papers are first sent to union members on 1 April 2017, they cannot authorise action taken beyond 1 October 2017. During this period the union will need to receive and count the ballots, notify the employer and eligible voters of the results, and give advance notice of the action to the employer.

New turnout and support thresholds
Fifty per cent turnout requirement for all ballots. New measures to prevent unions taking action where only a minority of members have engaged with the ballot process (and the number voting for action is therefore an even smaller minority), are one of the central planks of the new Trade Union Act, and may bring about the biggest changes in practice.

Whereas in the past, a "Yes" vote by a majority of those union members returning ballots was sufficient to authorise industrial action, at least 50% of all those entitled to vote must now do so for any resulting action to be authorised.

So, if 500 union members are affected by a dispute, at least 250 of those will now need to vote in order for the ballot to be valid. If 250 do vote, a simple majority of them will need to vote "Yes" for the ballot to validate industrial action (that would be 126 members assuming no spoilt, or invalid ballot papers). If all 500 voted, 251 would need to vote in favour (again assuming no spoilt, or invalid ballot papers).

Important public services. Even more stringent thresholds will apply for ballots covering union members engaged in "important public services"; under the new requirements 40% of all those entitled to vote must vote "Yes" to authorise any industrial action. So, if 800 union members are affected by a dispute, the 50% turnout threshold will first need to be met by at least 400 members returning a ballot.

The next test will be whether or not the dispute is within an important public service and, therefore, also subject to the 40% threshold. If so, at least 320 (40%) of the 800 members will need to vote "Yes" to enable industrial action (again subject to no spoilt, or invalid ballot papers).

Five sets of regulations defining "important public services" have also been published and are in force from 1 March 2017. They are narrower than many expected, especially in relation to health services. In brief, the important public services rules will cover:

Health: Vital medical services such as ambulance services, accident and emergency services in hospitals, high-dependency units and intensive care in hospitals, emergency psychiatric and obstetric and midwifery services.

Transport: London bus and passenger rail services (including maintenance and some station services, but not international rail services), air traffic control services, and airport and port security services.

Education: Teaching services (provided by teachers) at non-fee-paying schools, academies for students aged 16-19, and limited further education institutions.

Border security: Border control services, such as customs, patrol, inspection and intelligence services.

Fire: Firefighting services, and those handling calls to request services.

Private-sector union members in the fire, transport and border security services, and some limited health services, will be included in the threshold if they are delivering these services.

The existing rules on where unions may ballot more than one site together will continue to apply, but the new turnout thresholds will mean that where separate ballots are held, a union may not proceed with industrial action at any individual workplace where they have not all been met.

Where ballots do cover multiple sites, action will be lawful at any of the included workplaces if the thresholds are met in the aggregate.

Defining those eligible to vote is likely to become a matter of greater importance, and dispute under the new requirements, especially where important public services are involved. However, unions will still have a certain "margin for error", as they are required to ballot those they reasonably believe are entitled to vote, and a similar test will apply to engagement in important public services.

The Government has also produced practical guidance to accompany these Regulations.

Picketing supervisor. As a measure to tackle intimidation during strike action, it is now a requirement for a union to appoint a supervisor to oversee any picketing for picketing to qualify for protection. This will apply to picketing where notification is given to the employer from 1 March. The appointed picket supervisor must:

- Be an official, or member of the union who is familiar with the picketing code of practice.

- Take appropriate steps to tell the police their name, contact information, picket locations (or the union may provide this information).
- Be provided with a letter stating that the picketing is approved by the union, which must be shown to the employer on request.
- Be present where the picketing is taking place, or be able to attend at short notice.
- Wear something identifying them as the picket supervisor (such as a badge or armband).

The picket supervisor will be responsible for ensuring that the picketing is peaceful and complies with the code, and will be a visible point of contact for the employer and if necessary, police. Where two or more unions picket together, any one of those unions may appoint a supervisor. A revised code of practice on picketing has now been published, replacing previous versions and provides more detail on the requirements.

Political fund

The 12-month transition period for changes to union political funds began on 1 March 2017. Members joining after 1 March 2018 will need to opt in to make political contributions, and new funds set up after this date will also require opt-in. New guidance on political funds is now available to reflect the changes.

Unions must include detailed information about political expenditure when publishing returns for periods beginning after 1 March 2017.

From 10th March 2018, the Government will have the ability to regulate union facility time, and to make changes to "check off" provisions in the public sector, but no draft regulations have yet been published.

The Government announced an independent review of electronic voting for industrial action ballots in November 2016.

Future role of agency workers – Employment businesses are currently prohibited from providing agency workers to cover the duties normally performed by workers who are taking part in industrial action. However, the Conservative Party manifesto stated that it would seek to "repeal nonsensical restrictions banning employers from hiring agency staff to provide essential cover during strikes". Whilst a public consultation was carried out on this issue in 2015, no such proposals were brought forward as part of the Act. The outcome of the consultation has yet to be announced and could still result further changes in the future.

The Information and Consultation of Employees (ICE) Regulations 2004

Under the Information and Consultation of Employees (ICE) Regulations 2004, employees can request that the employee set up arrangements to inform and consult them. When a valid employee request is made, the employer is obliged to negotiate the details of an information and consultation (I&C) agreement with the representatives of employees.

What is a valid employee request?

If 10 per cent of employees request that the employer set up an I&C agreement, the employer is obliged to do so. That 10 per cent is subject to a minimum of 15 and a maximum of 2,500 employees.

To calculate the size of the work force, the employer should calculate the average number of employees in their business over the past 12 months. They can count part-time employees working under a contract of 75 hours or less a month as half of one employee for this calculation.

To be valid, an employee request must be in writing, dated and stating the names of the employees making the request. If they wish to remain anonymous, the employees may submit a request to the Central Arbitration Committee (CAC) who will inform the employer that a valid request has been received.

It is possible for a valid request to be made up of a number of different requests from different employees over a rolling six-month period, if this achieves the 10 per cent threshold.

Negotiating an I&C agreement

If the employer receives a valid employee request, they will need to make arrangements to begin negotiating an I&C agreement as soon as is reasonably practicable. They will need to arrange for their employees to elect or appoint a body of representatives to negotiate the agreement with them.

The employer must also inform their employees of the identity of the negotiating representatives in writing once this has been done. The employer will have six months to negotiate the agreement, starting three months from the date that they received the employee request. If they and the employees' representatives agree, they can extend this period indefinitely.

A negotiated agreement must cover all of the employees in the undertaking, If the employees and employer fail to reach an agreement, or do not start negotiations, fall-back provisions will apply. The employer can decide, in agreement with employees' representatives, the terms of a negotiated agreement. It should set out what is to be discussed, when it will be discussed and how often the discussion will take place. The areas on which are to be informed and consulted are for employer and employees' representatives to agree on.

The employer can also agree with the negotiating representatives whether I&C will take place through employee representatives or directly with the workforce. If the employer opts to use representatives, then provision should be made for employees to elect or appoint them. They do not have to be the same representatives as those that negotiated the agreement. Whilst trade union representatives do not have any special rights to act as an I&C representative, employees may decide to elect or appoint a trade union representative as an I&C representative.

The Certification Officer and Independent Trade Unions

The Certification Officer is the official who maintains a list of trade unions and can issue any union with a certificate of independence. Such a certificate is conclusive evidence that a union is independent. Section 5 of the Trade Union and Labour Relations (Consolidation Act) 1992 states that an independent union is one which is not under the control of an employer or liable to interference from an employer arising out of financial, material or other support. This definition was elaborated in the Court of Appeal and Squib UK Staff Association v Certification officer (1979).

Recognition of Trade Unions

The major purpose of any union is to protect and promote its members interests and the way it will do this is by collective bargaining. Recognised Trade Unions have certain rights. Recognised Trade Unions are entitled to information for collective bargaining purposes.

Union request for recogtnition

The union must ask the employer in writing if they agree to recognise them voluntarily. The written request must:
- give the name of the union

- identify which employees will be represented by the union when it's recognised, sometimes known as the bargaining unit
- state that the union is making the request under Schedule A1 of the Trade Union and Labour Relations (Consolidation) Act 1992

Respond to the request

The employer has 10 working days to respond to the request. They can:

- agree to recognise the union voluntarily - and begin collective bargaining
- reject the request - the union may then apply for statutory recognition
- refuse the initial request but agree to negotiate

Negotiate with the union

The employer has 20 working days, or longer if they agree this with the union, to come to an agreement about:

- which employees are in the bargaining unit
- whether the union should be recognised for collective bargaining

The employer has 10 days to suggest that the Advisory, Conciliation and Arbitration Service (Acas) are brought in to assist with the negotiations.

What happens next

If the employer can't agree, or they have agreed the bargaining unit but not recognised the union, the union can apply to the Central

Arbitration Committee (CAC) for statutory recognition. The CAC is a government body.

The Rule Book

The rules of a trade union form the terms of a contract between it and its members. They become part of a contract in the same way that collective agreements become part of the individuals employment contract between the employer and the employee. Apart from contract, other areas of law impact on the union rulebook. Statute has now impacted in a variety of ways. By s 69 of the Trade Union and Labour Relations (Consolidation) Act 1992, for example, there is a rule in union rulebooks allowing a member to terminate his membership on the giving of reasonable notice.

In addition, the Equality Act 2010 rendered it unlawful to discriminate on the grounds of race or sex, in relation to membership.

The Right to Information

The Employment Protection Act 1975 recognised that to be able to collectively bargain effectively, unions needed certain information from the employer and as such the Act introduced a right to receive certain information. This right has been retained and the provisions are now ss 181-5 of the Trade union and Labour Relations (Consolidation) Act 1992. The employer only has to disclose information in relation to those matters for which the union is recognised for collective bargaining.

ACAS has produced a code of practice (ACAS Code of Practice 2: Disclosure of information to Trade Unions for Collective Bargaining Purposes) which in paragraph 11 lists the type of information it would be good industrial relations practice to disclose. This includes pay and benefits, conditions of service, manpower, performance and financial information. Section 182 of the Act
186

provides restrictions on information that the employer does not have to disclose, such as information in the interests of national security. Section 183 provides a remedy for a trade union where the employer has failed to provide information. The remedy is complaint to the Central Arbitration Committee (CAC). Sections 184-185 further strengthen the complaints procedure.

The Closed Shop

There was no legal control over the closed shop until the Industrial Relations Act 1971. This Act introduced the concept of unfair dismissal. In 1988, the Employment Act 1988 rendered any dismissal for union or non-union membership unfair in any circumstances (now s 152 of the Trade Union and Labour Relations (consolidation) Act 1992. As such, while post entry closed shops can still exist, no one can be legally compelled to join a union.

The legislation of 1988 however, did nothing to prevent pre-entry closed shops operating, pre entry meaning insistence on membership of a union before being offered employment. The Employment Act 1990 finally destroyed any protection which existed for the pre entry closed shop by rendering it illegal to discriminate on the grounds of membership of a union prior to employment. This is now Ss 137-1243 of the Trade Union and Labour Relations (Consolidation) Act 1992.

Discipline of union members

Although expulsion from the union may be imposed as a disciplinary sanction, it is not the only form of sanction imposed by a union on its members. The courts insist however, that the union must comply with the natural rules of justice when exercising sanctions against a member. These are:

1. *Notice.* A person must be given adequate notice of the charge against him and the potential penalty so that he has an opportunity

187

to answer it. In Annamunthodo v Oilfield Workers Union (1961) the plaintiff knew that he was being charged with making allegations against the union presidents and knew he could be fined. He did not know that such conduct was treated as prejudicial to the union and that he could be expelled. It was held that his subsequent expulsion was void.

2. *Opportunity to put his case.* A person must be given the opportunity to put his side of the case and answer any charges against him.

3. *Unbiased hearing.* The hearing should be unbiased.

4. *Representation.* The rules do not specifically state that a person should be allowed legal representation and it appears from Enderby Town Football Club v Football Association (1971) that such representation can be specifically excluded by the rules as long as some kind of representative is allowed.

Action Short of Dismissal

The law affords a certain amount of protection against an employer. The law protects an employee who is dismissed for trade union membership or non-membership or for taking part in trade union activities at the appropriate time. Protection against dismissal is complemented by protection against action short of dismissal for one of the above grounds and is now found in s 146 of the Trade Union and Labour Relations (Consolidation) Act 1992. Should a tribunal find a complaint well founded it can make a declaration to that effect and award compensation to offset any loss caused by the action. In addition, either the complainant or the employer may join the union as a co-respondent if it was union pressure which induced the action and the tribunal can order that some or all of the compensation be paid by the union. Refusal to grant a benefit on these grounds is action short of dismissal for the purposes of protection. In NCB v Ridgeway (1987) it was held that refusal to give a pay rise negotiated with the UDM to NUM Members was unlawful action short of dismissal. In other words it is sufficient if the employer discriminates against members of a particular union and it is not necessary to show discrimination against union members as a whole.

Economic duress

All industrial action is intended to put pressure on the employer. In contact law, economic pressure can amount to duress and, if proved, the contract can be avoided and any money paid under it recovered. Normally this argument is not used against unions as they have no contract with the employer. However, in Universe Tankships of Monrovia v International Transport Workers Federation (1983) such a contract did exist. The Federation, as part of its campaign against flags of convenience, insisted that employers pay a sum into the union's welfare fund as the price for lifting the blacking of a ship. As soon as the blacking was lifted the employers sought to recover the money they had paid, arguing the payment had been made under duress and therefore was avoidable. The House of Lords said that if the action had been protected by the immunities, that is, if it was in contemplation or furtherance of a trade dispute, the employer could not circumvent the protection by bringing an action for duress. However, since payment into a welfare fund is not a recognised trade dispute, there was no such protection and the employer's action succeeded.

Statutory Immunities

It can be seen from the above that unions can commit a great number of economic torts when they take industrial action, but we have also seen that in some circumstances there will be statutory immunity from liability for the commission of certain torts. The

189

immunity is now contained in s 219 of the Trade Union and Labour Relations (Consolidation) Act 1992, which states: "An act done by a person in contemplation or furtherance of a trade dispute is not actionable in tort on the ground only –

a) that it induces another person to break a contract or interferes or induces another person to interfere with its performance or
b) that it consists in his threatening that a contract (whether one to which he is a party or not) will be broken or its performance interfered with, or that he will induce another person to break a contract or interfere with its performance.

It will be seen therefore that protection is not afforded against the commission of any tort and that such torts as libel and slander, trespass, breach of statutory duty and so on have no immunity.

Trade union liability
The 1906 Trade Disputes Act introduced immunity from tortious liability for trade unions. This blanket immunity was removed by the Employment Act 1982 and now a union has the same immunity as its individual members. There is a statutory limit on the damages that can be awarded against a union, first introduced in 1982 and now contained in s 22 of the 1992 Consolidation Act.

The 1992 Act states that the amount of damages depends on the number of members the trade union has. If there are less than 5,000 the maximum is £10,000. Between 5,000 and 25,000 the maximum is £50,000. Between 25,000 and 50,000 the maximum is £125,000 and over 100,000 the limit is £250,000. Each separate action may result in the maximum being imposed. Therefore, if more than one employer takes action against the union then the limit can be imposed separately for each employer. Furthermore, the limit only applies to damages and not for fines for contempt. Thus in the NGA
190

dispute against the Stockport messenger in 1984 the union was fined £675,000 for contempt.

Loss of trade union immunity

Trade Union Immunity depends on the protected torts being committed and the balloting and notice requirements being complied with. Breach of any of these conditions will render the union liable for any tortious wrongs committed. A ballot is required in respect of any act done by a trade union, that is, in respect of any action authorised or endorsed by the union. Entitlement to vote must be accorded to all members of the union who will be induced to take part in the action and the ballot will be ineffective if this provision is not complied with.

Picketing

Picketing is a method by which a trade union can strengthen a strike. It can prevent workers from entering the workplace and so increase the disruption to the employer. The problem with picketing from a legal point of view is that it involves a consideration of both the civil and criminal law. The criminal law becomes involved because the fact that picketing involves a group of people standing around can create criminal liability. In addition, pickets will normally interfere with contracts, be committing a trespass and often be committing a private nuisance, so rendering them potentially liable in tort. As such it is necessary to consider all the potential liability and look at the immunity. Criminal liability, for example may be committing the offence of obstructing the highway, obstructing a police officer during the course of his duty or causing a public nuisance generally.

Civil liability might be that of committing a private nuisance, which is unlawful interference with an individual's enjoyment of his land, trespass to the highway or general economic torts such as

191

breach of contract of employment. Immunity for pickets is contained in s 220 of the 1992 Act. This renders it lawful for a person, in contemplation or furtherance of a trade dispute, to attend at or near his own place of work for the purpose of peacefully obtaining or communicating information, or peacefully persuading a person to work or not to work. In addition, a trade union official may peacefully picket at or near the place of work of a member of the union whom he is accompanying or whom he represents. Unemployed employees are allowed to picket their former place of work if their employment was terminated in connection with the trade dispute or the dismissal gave rise to the trade dispute.

See section on the Trade Union Act 2016 above concerning changes to picketing. As outlined, the law requires any pickets to peacefully communicate their cause, including asking colleagues to refrain from working. New regulations implementing the Trade Union Act 2016 and an accompanying revised Code of Practice on Picketing (the Code) mean that as of March 2017, unions must appoint a named member or official as a picket supervisor for industrial action involving picketing.

The picket supervisor must be familiar with the Code, be equipped with a letter of authorisation and something to readily identify him/her. He or she acts as a point of contact to ensure that pickets are peaceful, do not cause obstruction, and are otherwise safe and in line with the Code. Without an appropriate picket supervisor, picketing will not be lawful, and the union responsible will not have the established protection from civil legal action.

Remedies against the union

Obviously, although the individual member commits the tort, it is more beneficial for an employer to sue the union, hence the removal of blanket union immunity in 1982. The majority of employers, however, do not want damages but rather want to prevent the

192

action from commencing or to stop it as soon as possible. The most common remedy sought is that of injunctive relief. If the union fails to comply with an injunction the two methods of enforcement are committal for contempt and sequestration of the union assets.

The court may imprison for contempt, fine or order security for good behavior.

The 2002 Employment Act-Union Learning Representatives

The 2002 EA, S.43 provides for time off for Union learning representatives. These provisions are similar to time off rights for Health and Safety Representatives. They allow time of for Union appointees, working in the interests of members of trade unions to:

- Analyse learning or training needs
- Provide information about or promote learning or training
- Arrange learning or training
- Consult with employers about any of the above

For more detailed advice on Trade Unions and the rights and obligations of employees and employers, plus the rights of citizens, go to www.gov.uk/browse/working/rights-trade-unions. This site gives detailed information about all aspects of trade unions, rights of employer and employee and the Trade union Act 2016.

In addition, for more detailed information about the 1992 Consolidation Act go to:

www.legislation.gov.uk/ukpga/1992/52/contents

Chapter 12

Solving Grievances-Tribunals and Arbitration

Before the advent of the industrial tribunal system in 1964, labour law was regarded as an aspect of the law of contract, dealt with by the civil courts. Since 1964, the industrial tribunal system has grown and now encompasses other courts and non-judicial bodies. Industrial tribunals were renamed Employment Tribunals by the Employment Rights (Dispute Resolution) Act 1998. The Employment Tribunals Act 1996 also regulates Employment Tribunals.

The 2002 Employment Act introduced significant proposed changes to the tribunal system along with the Employment Tribunals (Constitution and Rules of procedure) Regulations 2004. In addition, there have been Regulations issued in 2005 and 2008. The President of the Tribunal can also issue new directions from time to time. Further changes to the system, aimed at simplifying the procedure, and introducing the requirement to pay fees, (fees have now been abolished) were introduced in July 2013 and are outlined below.

Following changes which came into force in April 2014 anyone thinking about making an employment tribunal claim must contact Acas first. Acas then offers 'early conciliation' to try and resolve the dispute quickly and cost effectively. This builds on Acas experience with offering pre-claim conciliation in cases which seem likely to end up in the tribunal.

Employment Tribunals

Employment Tribunals (previously known as Industrial Tribunals) have jurisdiction to hear almost all individual disputes based on statutory employment law claims and, in addition, common law contract claims arising from or outstanding at the termination of employment.

An Employment Tribunal is normally comprised of three members: an ET Judge, being a barrister or solicitor of seven years standing; and two lay members, drawn from either side of industry, one having experience perhaps as a trade union official, the other having had management or trade association experience. Although it is not that common, it is possible for laypersons to outvote the legally qualified chair.

The tribunal system was set up with the aims that it should be quicker, cheaper, more efficient and more accessible than the normal court system. In many ways this has been successful, although delays in processing cases and becoming common, partly due to the increased use of legal representation, particularly by employers, which tends to slow the system down. It is usually recommended, before reaching the stage of going to an Employment Tribunal, that some sort of mediation in the workplace takes place to try to resolve disputes. If this avenue fails then it will usually be necessary to go to an Employment Tribunal. Failure to resolve disputes via mediation, or to attempt the mediation process will not affect rights when going to a Tribunal.

There are a number of advantages and disadvantages to the tribunal system and these include:

a) Informality, lack of ceremony etc. Hearings are normally conducted in a room, which although purpose built, is very similar to any meeting or function room.

195

b) Representation may be by the party themselves, a lawyer, trade union representative, a friend etc., although it should be noted that most companies tend to be legally represented.

c) Legal aid is not available for first instance tribunal hearings, but may be available for appeal hearings before the Employment Appeals Tribunal (EAT).

d) Costs are rarely awarded, thus there is no financial threat to an applicant bringing a claim.

e) The members of the tribunal are specialist and experienced in employment disputes. Unlike most magistrates or judges, members of an employment tribunal hear only cases within one area of law.

f) Certain rules of evidence, i.e. hearsay, do not apply.

Claims that can be heard by an Employment Tribunal

An Employment Tribunal can only decide cases that relate to specific rights. The range of complaints include:

- Unfair dismissal
- Discrimination on the grounds of disability, race etc.
- Not being allowed to have someone accompany you to a disciplinary or grievance procedure
- Not being consulted in a redundancy situation
- Breach of contract
- Equal pay

There are many others. A full list can be found by contacting ACAS.

The procedure for bringing a complaint before an Employment Tribunal is fairly straightforward. The applicant, following initial consultation with ACAS, who will offer a free conciliation service to

196

try to solve the dispute before going to a Tribunal, completes a form and sends it to the tribunal office. A copy of the form is then sent to the employer who has 14 days in which to respond. Both the original form and the employer's response are then copied and sent to the Advisory Conciliation and Arbitration Service (ACAS), who may then attempt to obtain a settlement between parties. If the claim is not settled at this stage, the tribunal will then make a preliminary examination of the case and may hold a pre-hearing review, often consisting of a tribunal judge sitting alone. This is in order to weed out particularly weak cases. Once a case goes to a full tribunal hearing the procedure adopted is similar in many ways to a court hearing, normally being open to the public. It is basically an adversarial procedure, with each party putting its case, witnesses may be called and examined and other evidence produced. However, unlike most other judges in court hearings, the members of the tribunal take a more active role in proceedings, questioning the parties and, if appropriate, leading applicants through the hearing procedure

It is now standard practice for the tribunal to give the reasons for its decision in summary form, rather than in extended form, although this does not apply to cases of equal pay or discrimination.

If the applicants claim is successful, the tribunal may award any of three remedies: reinstatement, re-engagement or compensation. The most often awarded remedy is compensation.

Fees

Since July 26th 2017, following a successful case by UNISON, there is now no longer a requirement to pay a fee to make a claim to the Employment Tribunal or Employment Appeals Tribunal.

Compensation

While there are exceptions, the most significant of which are discrimination and whistleblowing claims, for the most part the level of compensation that tribunals may award is subject to statutory limits. The limits from April 6th 2018 are as below;

- Unfair dismissal: cap on compensation awards rises to £83,682
- Basic award: minimum basic awards for automatically unfair dismissal (for health and safety, employee representative, trade union, or occupational pension trustee reasons) rises to £15,240
- Week's pay: cap rises to £508 This amount is used to calculate, for instance, redundancy pays and the basic award for unfair dismissal.
- Guarantee pay: rises to £28 per day for 5 days in any 3 month period. This rate is applied during times of lay-off or short-time working.

****

Further Information
Useful helplines and advice services

TUC Worksmart
Worksmart is the TUC's online information resource providing up to date information and advice on rights at work. This can be accessed via the TUC website wwwtuc.org.uk

http://www.worksmart.org.uk/

TUC Know Your Rights Line
This line will provide you with a range of information.
0800 917 2368

http://www.tuc.org.uk/tuc/rights_main.cfm

ACAS public enquiry points
The Advisory, Conciliation and Arbitration Service (ACAS) is a publicly funded body that promotes good workplace relations: ACAS has a number of advice lines across the country and these can be accessed through directory enquiries.

www.acas.org.uk

The Employment Tribunal Service
https://www.gov.uk/courts-tribunals/employment-tribunal

National Minimum Wage Advice and Guidance ACAS
acas.org.uk/nmw
Further information about the national minimum wage can be obtained from ACAS.hmrc.gov.uk

199

Low pay Commission

General enquiries 020 7211 8119

www.gov.uk/government/organisations/low-pay-commission

Discrimination advice

There are three public agencies that provide advice respectively on sex, race and disability discrimination. They not only provide detailed advice but are prepared to present individual cases. These are:

Equality and Human Rights Commission

www. equalityhumanrights.com

0808 800 0082

LAGER

Lesbian and Gay Employment Rights (LAGER) provides help, advice and tribunal representation for lesbians and gay men facing discrimination in the workplace: Unit 1G, Leroy House, 436 Essex Road, London N1 3QP 020 7704 6066 Email: lager@dircon.co.uk

The Discrimination Law Association can provide information on discrimination law and promotes access to representation for complainants www.discriminationlaw.org Tel: 0845 478 6375

Data protection

The Office of the Information Commissioner provides information and advice about the rights of individuals established under the Data Protection Act 1998 and the Freedom of Information Act 2000. tel: 0303 123 1113 www.ico.org.uk

Whistle-blowing

Public Concern at Work can provide advice on 020 3117 2420

http://www.pcaw.co.uk/

Agency Workers

The Department for Business, Energy and Industrial Strategy regulates employment agencies. Its helpline is 0207 215 5000.

The Recruitment and Employment Confederation (REC) on 020 7009 2100 or at www.rec.uk.com is the trade association for employment agencies. The REC will investigate complaints against those agencies affiliated to it.

Health and safety

The Health and Safety Executive information line on 0300 003 1747 can help with all health and safety issues at work. http://www.hse.gov.uk/

Working time

The Department for Business, Energy and Industrial Strategy workright number is 0207 215 5000. This helpline will provide information on the working time directive.

The law and advice agencies

The law society is the national body for solicitors. It can give details of local solicitors who can advise on employment matters. 020 7242 1222. www.lawsociety.org.uk

Tax credits and Benefits

You can apply for tax credits online at www.hmrc.gov.uk and this web site also provides extra information about tax credits. There is a special advice line to check your eligibility for tax credits or get a claim pack. There is a helpline for further advice 0345 300 3900.

Trade Unions

If you want to join or contact a trade union, you can phone the TUC Know Your Rights Line 0800 917 2368 or consult the worksmart website www.worksmart.org.uk

****

A Guide to Employment Law

Appendix 1

Employment law differences in Northern Ireland

NORTHERN IRELAND	GREAT BRITAIN
Qualifying period in order to claim unfair dismissal = 1 year	Qualifying period in order to claim unfair dismissal = 2 years
NI retains the statutory dismissal procedure and the grievance procedure requirements are now contained in the LRA Code of Practice	GB repealed all of the statutory dispute resolution procedures and replaced them with the ACAS Code of Practice
Collective redundancy consultation period where over 100 employees = 90 days	Collective redundancy consultation period where over 100 employees = 45 days
Public Interest Disclosure legislation (whistle -blowing) remains largely the same since 1999 but HAS mirrored GB 2013 reforms since 2016	In summer 2013 there were 4 significant areas of change to the whistle-blowing law – public interest test, vicarious liability, some extended coverage, reduction of compensation for bad faith
A tribunal applicant can proceed to industrial tribunal directly if that is what they want, but since 2016 they have been required to consider early conciliation	A tribunal applicant must first consider conciliation through ACAS before progressing
The law on compromise agreements and settlement processes remains as it was	Recent reforms in relation to "settlement agreements and protected conversations
The law on TUPE transfers remains as it was in 2006	There were 6 technical reforms to TUPE 2006 legislation in 2014
Fit for Work – national occupational health service does not extend to Northern Ireland	Fit for work – national occupational health service rolled out between 2014-2015
Arbitration as an alternative to going to industrial tribunal can be used in over 50 areas of claim	Arbitration as an alternative to going to industrial tribunal can be used in only 2 areas of claim (unfair dismissal and flexible working)
No back-stop limitation period for making backdated holiday pay calculations that have not included contractual non-guaranteed overtime	From 1/ 7/ 15 employment tribunal claims have limited backdated holiday pay calculations that have not included contractual non-guaranteed overtime to 2 years
There is no regulation of exclusivity clauses in zero hours contract in Northern Ireland	Exclusivity clauses in zero hours contracts have been banned since January 2016

Flexible working requests for all employees are via the existing statutory process under the Employment Rights (NI) Order 1996	Flexible working requests for all employees are via the ACAS guidance
There are currently no plans to reform the law on either trade unions or industrial action	Some reforms into trade unions record keeping and lobbying have already been introduced, and there are further reforms planned regarding strike ballot thresholds later in 2016

Index